GOD'S MAXIMUM

EXPERIENCE THE HIGHEST LEVELS ATTAINABLE

JERRY SAVELLE

Published by Jerry Savelle Ministries International
Crowley, Texas, U.S.A.
JerrySavelle.org

GOD'S MAXIMUM
ISBN 9 781939 934734

For additional information, please visit jerrysavelle.org, or email info@jsmi.org, or write to Jerry Savelle Ministries International, PO Box 748, Crowley, TX 76036, U.S.A. or to order copies of this book and other resources in bulk quantities, please contact us at 1-817-297-3155.

TABLE OF CONTENTS

CHAPTER 1

BELIEVE!

It was a dark time for the children of Israel. Threatened by a great multitude of warriors including the Ammonites, a pagan people who did not worship the God of Israel, the situation was bleak.

The Spirit of the Lord came upon Jahaziel and he said, *"Thus says the LORD to you: 'Do not be afraid nor dismayed because of this great multitude, for the battle is not yours, but God's'"* (2 Chronicles 20:15).

King Jehoshaphat responded immediately to the word of the Lord, leading the children of Israel in a time of worship and prayer. The following morning, Jehoshaphat made this decree: *"Hear me, O Judah and you inhabitants of Jerusalem: Believe in the LORD your God, and you shall be established; believe His prophets, and you shall prosper"* (2 Chronicles 20:20).

5

That very day, miraculously, the armies that had come to destroy Israel instead destroyed one another. The Bible says all had fallen to the earth dead. None escaped.

But then something interesting happened. When God's people went to take away the spoil, they found so much precious jewelry that it took them three days to gather it and carry it away.

Jehoshaphat's words, "*Believe in the Lord your God, and you shall be established; believe His prophets, and you shall prosper*" are as true for God's people today as they were when they were first spoken.

I'd been in full-time ministry for nearly ten years when Charles Capps prophesied about a future financial inversion. Here is an excerpt from that prophetic word:

> Financial inversion shall increase ... The economy shall go up and it will go down; but those who learn to walk in the Word, they shall see the prosperity of the Word come forth in this hour in a way that has not been seen by men in days past ... Yes, there's coming a financial inversion in the world's system. It's been held in reservoirs of wicked men for days on end. But the end is nigh. Those reservoirs shall be tapped and shall be drained into the Gospel of Jesus Christ ... you will see things you've never dreamed come to pass.

The word *inversion* refers to the act of inverting. To *invert* means "to turn upside down; to reverse in position, order, direction." In other words, a financial inversion is a turn-around in finances.

That's exactly what happened when Israel heeded the words decreed by Jehoshaphat: "Believe in the Lord your God, and you shall be established; believe His prophets, and you shall prosper." On the very same day those words were spoken, God's people experienced a financial inversion.

Charles Capps was not the first person God used to speak about a transfer of wealth. Here are the words of King Solomon as presented in The Passion Translation: *"The brightest and best, along with the foolish and senseless, God sees that they all will die one day, leaving their houses and wealth to others"* (Psalm 49:10–11).

The Bible also says, *"But the wealth of the sinner is laid up for the just"* (Proverbs 13:22 KJV). I remember the first time I read that verse. I was only three months into my walk with the Lord and thought those words were interesting. I had no idea the verse was talking about financial inversion.

What I did know was that I was one of the "just." The word *just* means "righteous." I also understood Proverbs 13:22 isn't in the Bible just to fill space. It is a prophetic word, a word that I took hold of immediately.

When I went to work for Kenneth Copeland many years ago, Carolyn and I and our girls lived in south Fort Worth. To get to the office, I drove down I-35, where I passed by a major local brewery.

Each day I'd roll down my window and declare in the direction of that brewery, "The wealth of the sinner is laid up for the just!" Then I'd roll my window up and go to work. On the way home each evening, I did the same thing.

Years later, upon returning to my own office after I'd preached at a meeting, my accountant said, "Brother Jerry, we got a strange offering today. We received a check from that brewing company on I-35."

At first, I thought the offering was probably from a brewing company employee who'd been saved. But when I looked at the check, it was from the brewing company—and it was a wonderful offering.

God said the wealth of the wicked is laid up for the just. The Amplified Bible, Classic Edition, says it this way: "*The wealth of the sinner [finds its way eventually] into the hands of the righteous, for whom it was laid up*" (Proverbs 13:22).

Even if all that wealth of those sinners is passed down to their own families, and passed again to their families, it will eventually end up in the hands of the righteous.

The Bible says, "*Wealth gotten by vanity will be diminished*" (Proverbs 13:11 KJV). This is how most of the wealth of the sinner has been acquired. In this instance, the word *vanity* means "pride, conceit, arrogance, vain pursuit." The Amplified Bible says that "*wealth [not earned but] won in haste or unjustly or from the production of things for vain or detrimental use ... will dwindle away out of the hands of the wicked.*" And where is it headed? Into the hands of the righteous.

THE MESSAGE paraphrase of Proverbs 13:22 says, "*Ill-gotten wealth ends up with good people.*" The Passion Translation says, "*The wealth of the wicked is treasured up for the righteous.*"

James issued this stern indictment of the ungodly rich:

> *¹Come now, you rich, weep and howl for your miseries that are coming upon you! ²Your riches are corrupted, and your garments are moth-eaten. ³Your gold and silver are corroded, and their corrosion will be a witness against you and will eat your flesh like fire. You have heaped up treasure in the last days.* (James 5:1–3)

Those words could have a twofold meaning. First, the way their riches are attained is coming to an end. Second, all that was heaped up is reserved for the just (the righteous) in the last days.

In other words, God says to the ungodly, *"Oh, you've been heaping it up. You have treasuries of wealth, but you're not going to enjoy it. In the last days, it will be taken from you."*

There is yet more truth to be revealed in the fifth chapter of James. He says, *"Indeed the wages of the laborers who mowed your fields, which you kept back by fraud, cry out; and the cries of the reapers have reached the ears of the Lord of Sabaoth"* (James 5:4). The word *Sabaoth* means "armies, hosts, angels."

By the Spirit of God, James declares that two cries go out. These two cries go out in the world today. First is the cry of the wages, or harvest, that's been held back from the righteous. Think about your own harvest. Have you reaped all of it so far? If the answer is *no,* then it is being held back. The Bible makes it clear that *"whatever a man sows, that he will also reap*" (Galatians 6:7). It is a violation of spiritual law not to reap what has been sown.

There is a second cry. That cry comes from the reapers, those to whom the harvest belongs. As used in James 5:4, the word *cry* does not indicate tears of sorrow. This cry is a bold command. In essence this cry says, "I want my harvest, and I want it now! My harvest doesn't belong to you, Satan. It doesn't belong to the wicked. I'm crying out for my harvest!"

At the same time, the harvest cries out, "Let me go! Let me get into the hands where I belong. Now release me!"

The reason most believers don't cry out for their harvest is this: if it doesn't come the hour after they sow, or before dark, or the next morning, they tend to forget about it. I often wonder how much harvest these people are entitled to, but they won't get it because they've given up on it.

According to the Word of God, the harvest is crying out and the people it rightfully belongs to should be crying out. When they do, God causes a *divine connection* that brings the harvest to their hands.

THE MESSAGE paraphrase of James 5:4 says the people "*cry out for judgment.*" This kind of judgment means "discerning right from wrong, good from evil, and correcting it." It's not right that our harvest remains in the hands of the wicked. It's not right that our harvest remains in the hands of Satan. God corrects this situation when we cry out for judgment.

WE HAVE ENTERED A NEW SEASON

When Charles Capps prophesied in 1978 about the coming financial inversion, that prophetic word did not have a specific time frame attached to it. But it did say, "Those that learn to walk in the Word, they shall see the prosperity of the Word come forth in this hour in a way that has not been seen by men in days past."

One thing I know with certainty is that I am one of those who have learned how to walk in God's Word. I've learned a lot about God's Word and prosperity in my more than fifty years of ministry. So have a lot of other believers. That's why it wasn't surprising when the Lord recently brought Brother Capps's prophecy to my remembrance.

And then He said, *"Tell the people—those who have learned to consistently walk in My Word—they are entering My Maximum, the highest level attainable."*

I fully believe we have entered that season. I also believe that it is up to each of us to cooperate with God's intended financial inversion and receive all that has been laid up for us.

So, what does God mean when He talks about the maximum and attaining the highest level? We find the answer in Jesus' parable of the sower. Speaking of seeds that had been sown, He said, *"⁸But others fell on good ground and yielded a crop: some a hundredfold, some sixty, some thirty. ⁹He who has ears to hear, let him hear!"* (Matthew 13:3–9).

We know, of course, that the seed in this parable represents the Word of God. But the principle of thirty, sixty, and hundredfold harvest is what I want to illuminate. According to God's principle of sowing and reaping, both thirtyfold and sixtyfold returns are excellent. But a hundredfold return is the maximum—the highest level attainable!

In modern vernacular, we don't use the terms *thirtyfold, sixtyfold,* or *hundredfold.* Instead of saying a *hundredfold,* we say a *hundred times*. Many Bible translations also say a *hundred times*. It doesn't make any difference to me which term is used because here's what the Lord said to me: "*Son, when you see the word hundredfold in your Bible, I want you to say maximum results.*"

Again, God's maximum results *are* the highest level attainable!

One of the things God taught me in the early days of my ministry was that a hundredfold was always His best. I've preached about the hundredfold consistently throughout my years in the ministry, and I've gotten a lot of flak about it. Even from so-called Word of Faith preachers who say, "You can't go around telling people they'll get a hundredfold."

Oh, really? Let's see what Jesus had to say about it in the familiar Bible story of the rich young ruler.

> *[17]Now as He was going out on the road, one came running, knelt before Him, and asked Him, "Good Teacher, what shall I do that I may inherit eternal life?" [18]So Jesus said to him, "Why do you call Me good" No one is good but One, that is, God. [19]You know the commandments: 'Do not commit adultery,' 'Do not murder,' 'Do not steal,' 'Do not bear false witness' 'Do not defraud,' 'Honor your father and mother.'" [20]And he answered and said to Him, "Teacher, all these things I have kept from my youth." [21]Then Jesus, looking at him, loved him, and said to him, "One thing you lack: Go your way, sell whatever you have and give to the poor, and you will*

> *have treasure in heaven; and come, take up
> the cross, and follow Me." 22But he was sad
> at this word, and went away sorrowful, for he
> had great possessions.* (Mark 10:17–22)

The man in this story had great possessions, but the truth Jesus revealed was that the man's possessions *had him* because he couldn't give away any of what he had. That's how we can always tell if we have possessions, or they have us. If we can't give away a possession, then it has us. But Jesus had more to say.

> 23*Then Jesus looked around and said to
> His disciples, "How hard it is for those who
> have riches to enter the kingdom of God!"*
> 24*And the disciples were astonished at His
> words. But Jesus answered again and said to
> them, "Children, how hard it is for those who
> trust in riches to enter the kingdom of God!
> 25It is easier for a camel to go through the eye
> of a needle than for a rich man to enter the
> kingdom of God.* (Mark 10:23–25)

I want to stop and point out what Jesus did *not* say. He did not say that it was impossible for those who have riches to enter the kingdom of God. He said it was hard. In other words, though it's hard for a person to lay aside his or her trust in riches and turn allegiance to God, it is not impossible. There are many rich people who have turned their allegiance to God, who have allowed Him to use their wealth in miraculous ways to accomplish His will. Now let's see what Jesus had to say about a hundredfold.

> [28]*Then Peter began to say to Him, "See, we have left all and followed You." So* **Jesus answered and said, "Assuredly, I say to you, there is no one who has left house or brothers or sisters or father or mother or wife or children or lands, for My sake and the Gospel's, who shall not receive a hundredfold now in this time**—*houses and brothers and sisters and mothers and children and lands, with persecutions— and in the age to come, eternal life. But many who are first will be last, and the last first.*" (Mark 10:28–30)

Keep in mind that Peter was a businessman, a fisherman by trade. The day he decided to turn away from his trade to follow Jesus was the best day he'd ever had in his fishing business. He caught such a load of fish that his nets broke and the boat began to sink. Peter was not a poor man, yet Jesus virtually promised him a hundredfold. When? *Now.* In this lifetime. We won't need a hundredfold when we get to heaven. We need it down here.

What could each of us do right now if we reaped a hundredfold harvest from all the seed we've sown? We could finance the Gospel throughout the world and not put even a dent in our reserves.

In the early days of our walk with the Lord, Carolyn and I didn't have much—except the debt I'd incurred before I came to the Lord. A tenfold harvest on our seed wouldn't have helped us. We *had* to believe for a hundredfold.

Whenever we sowed seed, regardless how little it was, we would decree, "Lord, we're believing for a hundredfold harvest on this seed!" It didn't happen overnight, but we began to experience what we'd decreed. And today, a hundredfold harvest is what we always expect.

We call it maximum harvest!

YOU'LL RECEIVE WHAT YOU BELIEVE

In October of 1981, Carolyn was with me in Charlotte, North Carolina, where I was preaching with Brother Kenneth Copeland. After one of the sessions, Carolyn and I went to our hotel room to rest before the evening session began.

She went into the bedroom to lie down, but I decided to remain in the living area and relax. I took off my suit and hung it in the closet and then put on my robe. I sat on the sofa, my feet propped on the coffee table as I leaned back and closed my eyes. Suddenly, the Shekinah glory filled the room.

I'd never had that experience before. The room was so filled with God's glory that I couldn't even see the furniture. And then the Lord appeared to me.

"*My people are in financial famine,*" He said. "*I'm going to reveal to you the keys that will bring them out, and I'll hold you responsible for sharing them.*"

I picked up a legal pad and a pen that I'd laid next to the sofa and, as the Lord spoke to me, I wrote down everything He said. It seemed as if He spoke for hours, but when I was able to look at my watch, I realized the visitation had taken only minutes.

Carolyn was then awakened, and when she came into the room she said, "What's happening in here?"

"I just experienced a visitation from the Lord," I told her. And then I read the notes I'd taken.

"Jerry, are you going to tell Brother Copeland about this?"

"No. He and I have worked together long enough that I know he'll pick it up in the Spirit. I won't have to tell him."

When Carolyn and I arrived at the meeting that night, we sat on the front row with the other speakers. Brother Copeland sang a couple of songs, and then he told us to open our Bibles, but he didn't tell us the book, chapter, or verse. After a few moments, he closed his Bible and said, "Jerry, God visited you today. Come tell us what He said."

I went to the podium and preached a message the Lord allowed me to title, "Sowing in Famine." At that time in 1981, the entire world was in a severe economic recession that began in 1980 and lasted until 1982. When the Lord appeared to me that afternoon, the first thing He said was, *"Your ministry is experiencing financial famine. I want you to apply the keys I'm going to give you and set an example for the body of Christ. I will bless you just like I blessed Isaac."*

So, I had everyone turn to Genesis 26:12: *"Then Isaac sowed in that land, and reaped in the same year a hundredfold; and the Lord blessed him."* Notice the Bible says Isaac reaped his harvest in the same year that he sowed it. The same year!

I remember saying to the Lord—not out loud, but in my spirit—"Lord, You *do* understand that it's October." He said, *"What difference does that make? I told you I want you to be an example for the people. Don't you think I can bless you with a hundredfold in the same year? Be in unto you according to your faith."*

At that time there were ten departments in my ministry, and each had its own financial account. In addition, Carolyn and I were believing to build a new house, and we had an account for that faith project. The Lord said, *"I want you to write a $1000 check from each of your departments and from your personal account. Sow them into Kenneth Copeland Ministries tonight."*

After I finished preaching, I shared what the Lord had instructed me to do, and then I publicly presented Brother Copeland with a total of $11,000. I said, "I'm sowing in famine just like Isaac did," and I challenged the people there to do likewise. What I didn't tell them was that in some cases, the $1000 representing each account was the last $1000 I had in them. Brother Copeland received my seed and then prayed over it. I knew I'd just sown seed in good ground.

The following week I was in a meeting with Kenneth Hagin in Tulsa. He'd not been present at the meeting in Charlotte. When he stepped to the microphone to open the meeting the first night, he said, "Brother Jerry, come up here. The Lord just told me to do something. I'm about to sow the largest seed I've ever sown."

When I joined Brother Hagin on the platform, he said, "The Lord just told me to give you my airplane." What he didn't know was that the week before I'd sown $1000 out of my aviation account into Brother Copeland's ministry, believing for my next airplane. Brother Hagin's airplane was worth $250,000—a pretty good return on a $1000 seed!

The following night, the second night of Brother Hagin's meeting, a couple came up to me and said, "When we left Canada to come here, the Lord told us to bring you this check for your television ministry. It's $100,000." I'd sowed $1000 out of my television account and reaped $100,000. Again, a pretty good return on my seed.

That kind of encounter occurred again and again over the next sixty days. By the end of December, we'd received into each account a hundred times what had been sown.

Though I began to experience a hundredfold return years ago, we are seeing a manifestation of Jesus's words in a greater way: *"Assuredly, I say to you, there is no one ... who shall not receive a hundredfold now in this time"* (Mark10:29–30). We have entered a new season when hundredfold testimonies will be commonplace. We have entered into that time for the maximum!

When people tell me that hundredfold doesn't work, I tell them it's too late to tell me that. Jesus said, *"According to your faith let it be to you"* (Matthew 9:29). If your faith can believe for thirtyfold, go for it. If your faith can believe for sixtyfold, go for it. And if your faith can believe for a hundredfold—God's maximum, the highest level attainable—then go for it. You will receive what you believe!

CHAPTER 2

HOW TO PREPARE FOR THE MAXIMUM

The word *prepare* means "to put things or oneself in readiness; to get ready." Some seven hundred years before the birth of Jesus, Isaiah prophesied these words about John the Baptist: *The voice of one crying in the wilderness: "Prepare the way of the Lord"* (Isaiah 40:3).

Jesus said, *"In My Father's house are many mansions; if it were not so, I would have told you. I go to prepare a place for you"* (John 14:2).

And John writes this in his revelation: *"Then I, John, saw the holy city, New Jerusalem, coming down out of heaven from God, prepared as a bride adorned for her husband"* (Revelation 21:2).

19

It is evident that the act of preparation is a vital component of God's kingdom, both on earth and in heaven. So, since we have both a prophetic word about a coming financial inversion and another that says God's people are entering God's maximum, how then do we prepare to receive all that God has for us?

The first thing we must do to prepare is to mix our faith with the prophetic word. The Bible says, *For indeed the Gospel was preached to us as well as to them; but the word which they heard did not profit them, not being mixed with faith in those who heard it* (Hebrews 4:2).

How do we mix our faith with the prophetic word? By *saying* what that word says about us. For instance, we should say, "I am entering God's maximum," or "I receive my financial inversion." Jesus said, *"For assuredly, I say to you, whoever says to this mountain, 'Be removed and be cast into the sea,' and does not doubt in his heart, but believes that those things he says will be done, he will have whatever he says"* (Mark 11:23).

We *will* have what we say, good or bad. We should *never* say things like "I don't believe that stuff about the maximum. That financial inversion thing won't happen for me." I often tell people that if they can't talk the Word of God, then they should buy a roll of duct tape and tape their mouths shut until they *can* talk the Word! Our words have power.

God gives us prophetic words to raise our expectations. That's what He did for me when I heard Him speak about the maximum, the highest level attainable. When I wrote down the prophetic word He spoke, my expectations went to another level.

The psalmist said, "*My soul, wait silently for God alone, for my expectation is from Him*" (Psalm 62:5). I have a right to expect God's prophetic word to come to pass in my life because that word came from Him. I expect a hundredfold return on every seed I sow because I've mixed my faith with God's prophetic word, just as I mix it with His written Word. The Bible says, *Now faith is the substance of things hoped for, the evidence of things not seen* (Hebrews 11:1). My faith gives substance to my expectation.

Paul's prayer for the believers in Colossae was *that you may walk worthy of the Lord, fully pleasing Him, being fruitful in every good work and increasing in the knowledge of God* (Colossians 1:10). God is pleased when His people are fruitful in every good work and increase in their knowledge of Him. To be fruitful in every good work is the same as achieving the highest level attainable, because bearing fruit brings glory to God.

Jesus confirmed this truth, saying, "*By this My father is glorified, that you bear much fruit*" (John 15:8). When we bear much fruit, reaching the highest level attainable by mixing our faith with the prophetic word, God receives glory. Why? Because we could never reach that level on our own. But Jesus said, "*If you can believe, all things are possible to him who believes*" (Mark 9:23).

The second thing we must do to prepare to receive the maximum is to sow seed. We must look for opportunities to sow, and then sow all we possibly can.

Carolyn and I get up each morning and say, "Lord, Your Word says in Galatians that we are to be mindful to be a blessing. Give us opportunities today to be a blessing, to sow seed in good ground." And then we declare that, according

21

to Mark 10:30, we shall receive a hundredfold now in this time. THE MESSAGE paraphrase says, *"They'll get it all back, but multiplied many times."*

Mark 10:30 is God's promise to us. We must never give up on our harvest because God never forgets a seed we've sown. David penned these words: *"May the Lord answer you in the day of trouble; may the name of the God of Jacob defend you; may He send you help from the sanctuary, and strengthen you out of Zion; may He remember all your offerings, and accept your burnt sacrifice"* (Psalm 20:1–3).

Years ago, the Lord said to me, *"Write these words in the margin of your Bible: God never forgets a seed sown."* In Genesis we find the account of God establishing the law of seedtime and harvest. He said, *"While the earth remains, seedtime and harvest ... shall not cease"* (Genesis 8:22). God always blesses the seed we sow.

What farmer sows an apple seed and expects a harvest of one apple? Or sows a seed of corn and expects only one ear of corn? When a farmer takes the time to prepare the soil and then plant his seed, he does so in expectation of a far greater harvest than the number of seeds he's sown.

WHEN YOU SOW YOUR SEED, BELIEVE GOD FOR MAXIMUM RESULTS AND THE HIGHEST LEVEL ATTAINABLE. NOTHING IS IMPOSSIBLE FOR GOD.

We learned in chapter 1 that Isaac sowed his seed, and in the same year reaped a hundredfold harvest. The Amplified Bible, Classic Edition, says, *"Then Isaac sowed seed in that land and received in the same year a hundred times as much as he had planted, and the Lord favored him with blessings"* (Genesis 26:12).

Notice that God also favored him with blessings—but what did that look like? The Bible goes on to say, "*¹³And the man became great and gained more and more until he became very wealthy and distinguished; ¹⁴he owned flocks, herds, and a great supply of servants, and the Philistines envied him*" (Genesis 26:13–14 AMPCE). All this because Isaac sowed seed in a time of famine.

THE MESSAGE paraphrase says, *Isaac planted crops in that land and took in a huge harvest* (Genesis 26:12). The word *huge* means "vast; extremely large; immense; immeasurable; boundless." Obviously, Isaac got back far greater than the number of seeds he'd sown. He experienced God's maximum, the highest level attainable—in the same year that he sowed.

So, as we prepare to receive God's maximum harvest, we understand that we must first mix our faith with the prophetic word. Then we must sow seed. But we are not to stop there. There is yet a third thing we must do: we must not allow our harvest to die in the field.

Jesus promised in Mark 10:30 that those who choose to follow Him shall receive a hundredfold. When? Now—in this time. If Isaac could reap a hundredfold in the same year, and Jesus said we could reap a hundredfold in this time, then we *can* reap a hundredfold. How then, do we prevent our harvest from dying in the field? We do it by faith.

Jesus said, "*According to your faith let it be to you*" (Matthew 9:29). The Amplified Bible, Classic Edition, says,

"According to your faith and trust and reliance [on the power invested in Me] be it done to you."

Webster's Dictionary 1828, Online Edition, defines *faith* as "to draw towards something desired." As an example, it says that faith is like a rope, or a cable, used to pull us toward a desired position. That's what faith does. It pulls us toward a desired result.

If we want to experience the maximum, we can't sow our seed and then walk away with the attitude of "Well, if it's to be, then it will be." No! We must pull ourselves to our harvest *by faith.* Jesus has already decreed that the hundredfold is ours. It is up to us to pull that promise into the here and now.

Jesus said, *"For assuredly, I say to you, if you have faith as a mustard seed ... nothing will be impossible for you"* (Matthew 17:20). THE MESSAGE paraphrase says, *"The simple truth is that if you had a mere kernel of faith, a poppy seed ... There is nothing you wouldn't be able to tackle."* A maximum, hundredfold harvest may *seem* impossible, but Jesus said, *"With men this is impossible, but with God all things are possible"* (Matthew 19:26).

Faith makes all things possible! Faith keeps our harvest alive in the field. By faith we *can* take possession of God's maximum harvest. By faith we *can* attain the highest level.

FAITH FOR YOUR HARVEST

As we exercise our faith for maximum harvest, we must never limit God according to the way He brings it to us, or through whose hands it comes. Jesus said, *"Give, and it shall be given unto you; good measure, pressed down, and shaken together, and running over, shall men give into your bosom"* (Luke 6:38 KJV). To give is to sow. Notice that the return on this seed comes from men.

Now let's look at one type of individual God has prepared for our harvest to come through. The Word of God says, *"The wealth of the sinner is laid up for the just"* (Proverbs 13:22 KJV).

I remember first experiencing this promise in the early days of my ministry, before our family moved to Texas. I had been in the military with a man whose family was quite wealthy. They owned a lot of businesses in Louisiana. The man was a sinner, and I'd witness to him. Though he wasn't interested in hearing about Jesus, he always wanted me to tell him what I was doing in the streets and jails of Shreveport, where I ministered to drug addicts, alcoholics, and prostitutes.

He'd say, "What's happening in your ministry?" I'd tell him the latest story about someone giving their life to Jesus and being set free. And then I'd ask him, "Why don't you receive the Lord?"

His usual response was, "Nah, I'm not religious. I don't want that religious stuff."

I'd say, "I'm not talking about being religious. I'm talking about a *relationship* with Jesus."

As always, he'd say, "That's okay for you, but I don't want it."

One day when we were talking, he asked me how I was funding my ministry. I said, "I just trust God."

"What do you mean by that?" he asked.

I explained, "The Bible says, *'Give and it will be given to you, good measure pressed down, shaken together, and running over.*' I give to others, and I trust God to give to me in return."

He thought about my answer, and then leaned toward me and asked, "Does it happen?"

"I'm not a wealthy man by any means. I'm still believing to pay off my old business debts so that I don't have that burden. But God always meets my needs. He puts food on the table and gas in the car."

One day the man called me and asked me to come to his office. When I arrived, he said, "I don't know why I'm doing this…" (I always love it when someone says that to me. I know I'm about to experience some favor!) "But I feel that I'm supposed to give you some money."

He reached into his pockets, pulled out some cash, and handed it to me, saying, "Here." Then he went to his briefcase, opened it, pulled out some more cash, and gave it to me. Finally, he sat down and wrote a check for some more. As he handed me the check, he said, "I don't know why I'm doing this? Do you know why I'm doing this?"

I smiled and said, "Yes, I know why you're doing this. The Bible says the wealth of the sinner is laid up for the just. I'm the just and you're the sinner."

"Is that really in the Bible?"

"Yes, it is. I'll show you." I opened my Bible and pointed to Proverbs 13:22. He read it and then I said, "If you don't get saved, I'm going to end up with everything you've got!"

He got down on his knees and said, "Pray!" And then he made Jesus His Savior and Lord.

I lost track of that man when Carolyn and I moved to Texas. But several years ago, I ran into him in a restaurant. He said, "You know, I remember when you prayed for me in my office, and I got saved. I've been a deacon in our church ever since, and my life has never been the same."

I laughed and said, "Do you realize you were my first partner in my ministry? You were the first person who gave money to me."

"Well, Brother Jerry," he said, "That seed I sowed sure paid off. God has since blessed my business—big time!"

Not only did the wealth of the sinner end up in the hands of the just all those years ago, but that man also gave his life to Jesus. Today, not only is he serving God and others, but he continues to reap a harvest that began with that first seed he sowed. Praise God for the harvest!

I also remember the time when Oral Roberts was believing for money for a specific need at Oral Roberts University. He needed $8 million to pay off student loans for young doctors and nurses who had graduated, and whom he wanted to get onto the mission field.

He called me one day and asked if I'd come to Tulsa and join him in the prayer tower at ORU. He said, "Jerry, we already have most of the money, but we're down to the last million dollars and I want you to come pray with me."

I flew to Tulsa the next day, and when I got to the prayer tower, Brother Roberts was talking with a man that I didn't know. Brother Roberts introduced the man, and then explained who he was. "Jerry, this man came here from Florida, where he owns a dog racing track. He was watching my television program a few days ago and heard me say we were believing for the last million dollars to pay off the student loans.

"He told me he turned to his wife and said, 'Why aren't Christians paying this debt so the doctors and nurses can go to the mission field? We're not Christians, but I'm going to take care of that debt!'"

Then Brother Roberts smiled at me and said, "He just brought me the last million dollars that we needed."

The three of us prayed over that million-dollar check, and then the man left. I said, "Well, Brother Roberts, since you've got that last million, I guess I can go on home."

He said, "Yes, you can." But just as I opened the door to leave, he added, "Jerry, be sure to pray for those dogs!"

That's another example of the wealth of the sinner being laid up for the just.

Never say, "I don't know *how* God is going to get my harvest to me." God has more ways than we could ever imagine of making it happen.

IT'S JUST A MATTER OF TIME

The book of Deuteronomy not only summarizes the law and looks back at lessons from the past, but it also looks ahead with hope to God's promises. In chapter 8 we find the prophetic words that describe maximum results.

> *"⁶Therefore you shall keep the commandments of the LORD your God, to walk in His ways and to fear Him. ⁷For the LORD your God is bringing you into a good land, a land of brooks of water, of fountains and springs, that flow out of valleys and hills; ⁸a land of wheat and barley, of vines and fig trees and pomegranates, a land of olive oil and honey; ⁹a land in which you will eat*

> *bread without scarcity, in which you will lack nothing; a land whose stones are iron and out of whose hills you can dig copper. ¹⁰When you have eaten and are full, then you shall bless the LORD your God for the good land which He has given you.*
>
> *"¹¹Beware that you do not forget the LORD your God by not keeping His commandments, His judgments, and His statutes which I command you today, lest—when you have eaten and are full, and have built beautiful houses and dwell in them...* (Deuteronomy 8:6–12)

I want you to pay close attention to the final sentence in this portion of Scripture. Notice it says, *"When* you have eaten and are full." It does not say, *"If* you have eaten and are full." In other words, all the things described in the first paragraph *will* happen. It's just a matter of time until we experience all God has for us if we keep His Word.

Some may read that final phrase, "When you have eaten and are full, and have built beautiful houses and dwell in them," and say, "I don't believe anyone ought to have more than one house." Really? God did not say, "When you have built a beautiful house and dwell in it." He said *houses.* Let's continue reading Deuteronomy 8.

> *¹³And when your herds and your flocks multiply, and your silver and your gold are multiplied, and all that you have is multiplied; ¹⁴when your heart is lifted up, and you forget*

the LORD your God who brought you out of the land of Egypt, from the house of bondage, [15]who led you through that great and terrible wilderness, in which were fiery serpents and scorpions and thirsty land where there was no water; who brought water for you out of the flinty rock; [16]who fed you in the wilderness with manna, which your fathers did not know, that He might humble you and that He might test you, to do you good in the end—[17]then you say in your heart, 'My power and the might of my hand have gained me this wealth.' [18]And you shall remember the LORD your God, for it is He who gives you power to get wealth, that He may establish His covenant which He swore to your fathers, as it is this day. (Deuteronomy 8:13–18)

In the Old Testament, if God's people obeyed His commandments and walked in His ways, they could acquire wonderful blessings. But they were to remember that it was the Lord their God who made it happen. Their results didn't happen by the power of their own hands, might, or ability. It was God who enabled them to accomplish all these things.

Well, praise God, we have a better covenant founded upon better promises. If God's people could have tremendous results under the Old Covenant, we can have maximum results under the New Covenant.

The Word of God says, "*The blessing of the LORD makes one rich, and He adds no sorrow with it*" (Proverbs 10:22). And in Psalm 3:8 we find this promise: "*Your blessing is upon Your people.*" God's blessing has the potential of making a person rich. If you consider yourself one of God's people, then you have the potential to become rich. Of course, whether you tap into it or not is up to you. But the potential is there because God's blessing is upon you.

In the book of Genesis, we see the account of God making mankind in His image and pronouncing His blessing upon them: *Then God blessed them, and God said to them, "Be fruitful and multiply; fill the earth and subdue it; have dominion ... over every living thing that moves on the earth"* (Genesis 1:28). God wants each of us to live a blessed life, and a fruitful life of multiplication.

Don't be afraid to be rich. To be rich is to have your own needs met with enough left over to help others meet their needs. Can you imagine what would happen if every member of the body of Christ achieved maximum harvest on the seed he or she had sown, and lived at the highest level attainable?

The body of Christ would prosper to the point where we could fulfill God's plans and purposes throughout the entire world.

CHAPTER 3

THE PURPOSE OF PROSPERITY

I'd just finished preaching at the dedication of a small West Texas church when the pastor approached me and handed me an envelope. "Now, Brother Jerry," he said, "I don't want this offering to go into your ministry. This offering is for you and Carolyn *personally*. It's in appreciation of your work for the Lord and all you've done for this church."

When I opened the envelope before making the drive home to Fort Worth that night, I found $1000 cash inside, a significant amount at that time. Unless directed otherwise, all offerings went directly into my ministry account. Every employee of the ministry, including me, was paid a fixed salary determined by the board of directors. I smiled as I got into my vehicle, imagining the joy this extra money would bring to Carolyn. Of course, I could think of a few things I needed that I could purchase immediately.

It was almost 1 o'clock in the morning when I arrived home. I was surprised when Carolyn met me at the door. "Jerry, there's a family in town that's being evicted from their house right now. Their furniture is on the sidewalk. They have no money, no place to go, and they don't know what to do. They need a thousand dollars."

I said, "Carolyn, I have a thousand dollars in cash right now. Let's go!"

Carolyn told me the address, and when we arrived a short time later, I was stunned at what I saw. Three small children sat huddled together in the yard, clinging to their stuffed toys as their parents loaded furniture onto a trailer. That's when the Lord spoke to me and said, "Son, this is the reason I had that pastor give *you* the thousand dollars. This is where I want it to go. That money will allow this family to remain in their home."

Carolyn and I were willing to pass along the blessing God had given us that night. The couple paid their landlord the money due, and he allowed them to move back in. But that's not the end of the story. They learned the biblical law of sowing and reaping, and as they put it to practice God blessed them. They eventually became partners with *Jerry Savelle Ministries* sowing seed into our outreaches and being a blessing to others.

I'll never forget the way I felt that night. Of all the things I could have purchased with that money, nothing could have compared with the joy I experienced in being an instrument of God used to help that family in their time of need.

The events of that day had a profound impact on my life and ministry. I knew God wanted to bless and prosper us, for the Bible says, *"Beloved, I pray that you may prosper in all things and be in health, just as your soul prospers"* (3 John 1:2). It also says, *A good man leaves an inheritance to his children's children* (Proverbs 13:22).

God doesn't want us to have the bare minimum of what we need to get by, to meet only our own needs. No! He wants us to have plenty to give to help meet the needs of others, with enough left over to leave an inheritance for our two succeeding generations. The purpose of our prosperity is that we may be a blessing to others!

When I began to learn these Bible truths I was not yet at the level of prosperity where I could leave an inheritance to two generations. But I am today, and so are many other believers who have received God's Word and applied these principles in their lives.

This level of prosperity is available to anyone willing first to align his or her way of thinking with God's way of thinking where prosperity is concerned, and then use their faith to move to the highest level attainable.

In *our* dispensation of God's maximum, God is raising up some modern-day Abrahams, men and women who are blessed and will be a blessing to the families of the earth. Some may wonder, *How could God bless me so that I could bless that many people?* Well, if the unsaved heavyweight champion of the world can go into the boxing ring and earn $30 million in ninety seconds, then surely God can supply His children with enough money to bless millions of people around the globe.

When I made that point in one of my meetings, a man came to me and said, "Wait a minute, Brother Jerry. Are you saying we're all going to earn millions of dollars in a matter of minutes?" Of course not. But I believe more of us will experience all God has for us in this generation because it's part of His plan for the salvation of the world.

God is transferring the wealth of the sinner to the righteous so that we can proclaim the Gospel throughout the world as Jesus commanded. You and I are responsible to get the Gospel to the billions of people worldwide who have not yet heard it.

God wants us to prosper, but He doesn't want us to allow money to come between us and Him. He doesn't want us to buy into the mistaken idea that it's impossible to have money and at the same time serve Him.

Abraham had riches *and* he served the Lord, as did his son Isaac. So did many others in the Bible. Without riches, they could not have accomplished all that God had called them to do. Likewise, without prosperity we cannot do what God has called us to do.

Some may be quick to point out Proverbs 1:32: *"The prosperity of fools shall destroy them"* (KJV). This statement is true, but you and I are not fools. We are the wise sons and daughters of God. As children of the King, we have enough sense to know how to handle our heavenly Father's estate.

While fools are destroyed by prosperity, we have access to the wisdom and knowledge of God. The Holy Spirit will show us how to use prosperity wisely for God's purposes, for the salvation of souls. Here's what Paul said about God's purpose for prosperity:

¹⁰For God who gives seed to the farmer to plant, and later on, good crops to harvest and eat, will give you more and more seed to plant and will make it grow so that you can give away more and more fruit from your harvest. ¹¹Yes, God will give you much so that you can give away much. (2 Corinthians 9:10-11 TLB)

Our television broadcast is currently aired worldwide via cable television, satellite, and the internet. When God initially gave me the assignment to produce a program and air it throughout the world, the very idea was staggering. The personnel and money required to accomplish such a vision made it seem impossible.

But the Bible says, *"For with God nothing will be impossible"* (Luke 1:37). When I reminded myself that God is El Shaddai—not El Cheapo—I became excited about the possibilities and the vision He'd given me.

The Lord showed me that to help set the stage for the events that need to occur in the earth before the return of Jesus. There are some things He needs us to take hold of. One of these things is the medium of television.

The Word of God tells us, *All things were made through Him, and without Him nothing was made that was made* (John 1:3). Television was not created for any of the diabolical acts displayed there daily. Television was made for God, to preach the Gospel to the masses.

So how do we take control of television? Well, according to Proverbs 13:22, the wealth of the sinner is laid up for the just. In other words, God will deliver it into our hands.

The Bible also says, *"For the earth will be filled with the knowledge of the glory of the LORD, as the waters cover the sea"* (Habakkuk 2:14). How can the earth be filled with the knowledge of the Lord's glory without a means to do so? God intends for His people to access the avenue to get this knowledge to the world.

God has allowed mankind to progress technically, scientifically, mechanically, and electronically for the sole purpose of using these fields to transmit the knowledge of His glory. These marvels were created for Him, and for our use in serving Him.

Airplanes were not made for sinners. Jumbo jets weren't invented so that the "jet set" could peddle sin throughout the world. God intends for aircraft, both large and small, to be used for the sake of the Gospel. Some people grumble because their pastor drives a nice car. What will they think when he owns a 747 and takes the future congregation into a nation to share the Gospel?

If that idea stretches your thinking, you should probably spend more time with God. He is a big thinker who knows no limitations. And that's exactly what we should be too!

Jesus was a messenger of good news, but there were limitations on the number of people He could reach with His message. He could be in only one place at a time. If He preached in a synagogue in Nazareth, only those present could hear Him. If He went to Capernaum, He was limited to speaking to the people who were there.

But Jesus said, *"Most assuredly, I say to you, he who believes in Me, the works that I do he will do also; and greater works than these he will do, because I go to My Father"*

(John 14:12). The greater works done today are without the limitations Jesus experienced during His earthly ministry.

As members of His body, we all are to carry the good news into the world, whether in full-time ministry or in our individual areas of influence. We have access to television, the internet, and modes of transportation that didn't exist a century ago. We have access to these kingdom assets to use for God's purposes. All that is required is that we seek His kingdom and allow Him to be first place in our lives.

THINGS FOLLOW THE SEEKER

One of the blessings of obedience listed in Deuteronomy 28 is this promise: *"And the LORD will grant you plenty of goods"* (verse 11). It is important to understand that this blessing is *granted* by God.

We are not to pursue things. Jesus said, *"Seek first the kingdom of God and His righteousness, and all these things shall be added to you"* (Matthew 6:33). According to Deuteronomy 28:2, God's blessings will come upon us and overtake us—if we obey Him!

Those who are critical of the biblical message of prosperity say we preach and practice the pursuit of prosperity. But they are incorrect. We preach and practice the pursuit of God. He is the one who promised blessing and prosperity to those who seek Him and His righteousness. We expect the Lord to keep His Word. When He keeps His Word and blesses us with more than enough to meet our own needs, we are then equipped to help others as we carry out His will in the earth.

I want the blessed life God has promised me in His Word: *"And the LORD will make you the head and not the tail;*

39

you shall be above only, and not be beneath" (Deuteronomy 28:13). But that is not all this verse says. It comes with this condition: *"if you heed the commandments of the LORD your God, which I command you today, and are careful to observe them."*

Let's back up and see what else the Word of God promises us in Deuteronomy 28:

> ¹*Now it shall come to pass, if you diligently obey the voice of the LORD your God, to observe carefully all His commandments which I command you today, that the LORD your God will set you high above all nations of the earth.* ²*And all these blessings shall come upon you and overtake you, because you obey the voice of the LORD your God:*
>
> ³*Blessed shall you be in the city, and blessed shall you be in the country.* ⁴*Blessed shall be the fruit of your body, the produce of your ground and the increase of your herds, the increase of your cattle and the offspring of your flocks.*
>
> ⁵*Blessed shall be your basket and your kneading bowl.*
>
> ⁶*Blessed shall you be when you come in, and blessed shall you be when you go out.*⁷*The LORD will cause your enemies who rise against you to be defeated before your face; they shall come out against you one way and flee before you seven ways.*

> *⁸The LORD will command the blessing on you in your storehouses and in all to which you set your hand, and He will bless you in the land which the LORD your God is giving you.*
>
> *⁹The LORD will establish you as a holy people to Himself, just as He has sworn to you, if you keep the commandments of the LORD your God and walk in His ways."*
> (verses 1–9)

Those are some powerful promises of blessing, none of which God's people were to pursue. The blessings came to the people because of their obedience. The Scripture goes on to say, *¹⁰Then all the peoples of the earth shall see that you are called by the name of the LORD, and they shall be afraid of you. ¹¹And the LORD will grant you plenty in goods"* (verses 10–11). Verse 11 in the New International Version says, *"The LORD will grant you abundant prosperity."*

Abundant prosperity is God's will for His people as a sign to all the peoples of the earth of His blessing and His goodness!

When we experience God's abundant prosperity—especially when we are functioning at the highest level attainable—not only are our needs met, but we also have enough to help others in need. Such are the blessings of the covenant God made with His people, the descendants of Abraham. The Bible tells us that *we* are the descendants of Abraham: *"If you are Christ's, then you are Abraham's seed, and heirs according to the promise"* (Galatians 3:29).

41

The promise referred to in this verse is the promise that God will meet our every need: spiritual, physical, and material. Because of who we are in Jesus Christ, we can expect God to grant us abundant prosperity.

Abundant prosperity is not the only promise God made to Abraham. When God called him to leave his country, He said, *"I will make you a great nation; I will bless you and make your name great; and you shall be a blessing ... And in you all the families of the earth shall be blessed"* (Genesis 12:2–3).

The heritage of God's people is to be blessed and to be a blessing to all families (or nations) of the earth.

BLESSED TO BE A BLESSING

Just as it was God's original intent that His people be a blessing to all the families of the earth, so it is today. In modern vernacular, God says to us, "If you will seek Me and obey My voice, I'll see to it that not only are you blessed with abundant prosperity, but you'll also be a blessing to multitudes of others."

The Apostle Paul understood the "blessed to be a blessing" principle. He said, *"I realize that I really don't even need to mention this to you, about helping God's people. For I know how eager you are to do it, and I have boasted to the friends in Macedonia that you were ready to send an offering a year ago. In fact, it was this enthusiasm of yours that stirred up many of them to begin helping"* (2 Corinthians 9:1–2 TLB).

Paul went on to say, *"For God, who gives seed to the farmer to plant, and later on good crops to harvest and eat, will give you more and more seed to plant and will make it grow so that you can give away more and more fruit from your harvest* (verse 10 TLB).

These verses show us that God's covenant with us is twofold. First, if we are willing to seek and obey Him, He will bless us. Second, He will cause us to be a blessing to many others. In other words, God's blessings will come upon and overtake us so that we can pass them along to meet the needs of others.

To be a blessing to others means that we are instruments of God's divine favor. The topic I've preached more than any other throughout my more than fifty years in ministry is the favor of God. Here is how I define favor:

- Something granted out of goodwill
- A gift bestowed as a token of regard love, or friendliness
- Preferential treatment
- To have an advantage

It is both an honor and a blessing to be chosen by God to administer His favor in the life of others. **Oftentimes the administration of His favor prevents misfortune or catastrophe**—as in the story I told at the beginning of this chapter.

Sadly, many believers have yet to learn this truth. They think God's blessings are solely for their benefit, to meet their needs only. Of course, having plenty left over makes them happy. But for the wrong reason. They use the blessing to satisfy their own desires instead of helping others. This is not God's plan and purpose for the blessing.

It is both selfish and unscriptural to ask God to give us wealth and riches to consume upon our own desires. When we desire and pray for enough to meet our own needs *and* have plenty in addition to give to help someone else, God will honor that prayer. That prayer is in line with His will. It's part of His plan.

Jesus had the reputation of being a giver. He didn't come into the world to take from it. He came to give, saying, *"For even the Son of Man did not come to be served, but to serve, and to give His life a ransom for many"* (Mark 10:45). Jesus gave His life for us so that we can give our lives to Him.

Now let me speak directly to you. God doesn't want only part of you. He wants all of you, and everything you possess, to be available to Him to use to bless others.

Some believers have the mistaken notion that God doesn't want them to have anything. Religious tradition has led them to believe they have to be poor if they truly want to serve God, that they must give away everything they have.

This is not true. When God asks us to give, it is because He has something He wants us to receive. He wants us to be blessed so that we can be a blessing to others. We are blessed by God because we *need* to be blessed, to be instruments of God in someone else's life. Nothing can compare to being an instrument of God to help deliver someone out of bondage.

I've experienced in my own life the truth of Jesus words when He said, *"It is more blessed to give than to receive* (Acts 20:35). There is no greater joy in life than to *be* a blessing to someone in need.

CHAPTER 4

GOD ALWAYS HAS SOMETHING BETTER

I learned many years ago that when God asks me to let go of a possession—to give it away, to sow it—He isn't trying to take it from me. Rather, He plans to give something to me.

Giving and receiving is a principle of God's kingdom. It is how God does things. Jesus said, *"Give, and it will be given to you. A good measure pressed down, shaken together, and running over, will be poured into your lap"* (Luke 6:38 NIV).

I now know that when I'm prompted to give something away, it's time to expect something better.

Years ago, Carolyn and I purchased some acreage that had a little farmhouse on it. I'm a country boy and I like my space. We added onto the farmhouse and built a barn and

45

stables for our horses. There wasn't another house within sight, only fields. I was living my dream.

At that time, our ministry leased space in an office building. One day as I was contemplating the amount of money I paid in lease payments, I thought, *I'd rather pay for my own facilities instead of paying for someone else's building.*

We started looking for land on which to build but couldn't find a piece of property that met our needs. We looked in the area where we lived, but we couldn't believe the price for undeveloped land. As I was standing in my front yard enjoying the view one afternoon I thought, *Carolyn and I must be sitting on a gold mine out here.* That's when she and I began to pray about building our ministry headquarters on our property.

It turned out that we donated our property to the ministry, including the house we had just expanded and all the buildings. The only portion we retained was two acres, where we planned to build a house right next door to the ministry. With that donation, we became the largest contributors to *Jerry Savelle Ministries* at that time.

Let's look again at what Jesus said. *"Assuredly, I say to you, there is no one who has left house or brothers or sisters or father or mother or wife or children or lands, for My sake and the Gospel's, who shall not receive a hundredfold now in this time—houses and brother and sisters and mothers and children and lands, with persecutions—and in the age to come, eternal life"* (Mark 10:29–30).

I want to address a question I've been asked many times about the hundredfold return. People will ask, "Do you mean to tell me Jesus promised that if I give my house away, I'll get a hundred houses?" Or "So, are you saying that if I give my car away, I'll get a hundred cars?" The answer is *no*—but how about a house or car a hundred times better than the one given away?

The Lord explained it to me like this: "*When you see the word **hundredfold**, think of it as maximum results, the highest level attainable.*"

The point I want to make is that any time we sow a seed, we should focus on the expected return coming to us pressed down, shaken tother and running over. God always multiplies the seed we sow. Someone may say, "But, Brother Jerry, the Bible says we are to seek first God's kingdom and all these things will be *added* to us." That's true. But simply adding to the five loaves of bread and two fish the little boy in Matthew 14 gave to feed the crowd of five thousand wouldn't have fed everyone.

It took *multiplication* to meet that need. God's addition is always good, but I like His multiplication better.

When Carolyn and I donated our home to the ministry all those years ago, we subsequently received one far better than the one we'd given away. Not only did God bless us with a better home, but He also blessed us with a second home much nicer than anything we'd had before.

According to Jesus, when we are willing to give for His sake and the Gospel's, we are entitled to receive a hundredfold—God's maximum, the highest level attainable—now, in this time.

FAITH FOR THE HIGHEST LEVEL

Jesus said, *"For assuredly, I say to you, if you have faith as a mustard seed, you will say to this mountain, 'Move from here to there,' and it will move; and nothing will be impossible for you"* (Matthew 17:20).

Can you believe for the highest level attainable? Of course, the highest level for one person may be different from that of another. The reason is that one may have developed his or her faith more than the other.

When I first started in ministry, I couldn't imagine doing the things at my level of faith that Oral Roberts was then doing. He had been walking with the Lord and in ministry for many years. But I learned that I could get to that level, because faith comes by hearing and hearing by the Word of God (see Romans 10:17).

The more I fed my spirit the Word of God, the higher and stronger my faith became. My level of faith is now far greater than it was in 1969. It has grown.

This is the reason that what's attainable for one believer may not yet be for another believer. We each use our faith to receive the highest-level results that we can believe for. We always move upward, from one level of faith to the next. That's why Jesus said, *"According to your faith let it be to you"* (Matthew 9:29).

In God's economy, He doesn't just bless us back in equal measure to what we are willing to sow. He multiplies it back to us. The Bible says, *"⁷You must each decide in your heart how much to give. And don't give reluctantly or in response to pressure. 'For God loves a person who gives cheerfully.' ⁸And God will generously provide all you need. Then you will always have everything you need and plenty left over to share with others"* (2 Corinthians 9:7–8 NLT).

Carolyn and I believed to be debt free for many years, and we achieved that goal. Today our largest household expense is our giving—praise God! We don't pay a note on a house. We don't pay a note on a car. Everything we own is debt free. I call that abundant living.

Jesus said, *"I have come that they may have life, and that they may have it more abundantly"* (John 10:10). The Amplified Bible, Classic Edition, says, *"I came that they may have and enjoy life, and have it in abundance (to the full, till it overflows)."* When we live this kind of abundant life, we can sow our seed and then reap a harvest that enables us to bless others in a way that prevents misfortune in their lives. But we must be willing to sow.

For some in the body of Christ, getting out of debt is the level they want to attain. How, exactly, will God get them out of debt? The same way He got me out of debt—I sowed my way out!

In the natural, Carolyn and I couldn't afford to sow. This statement was a fact at that time, but it was not the truth. The truth was, we couldn't afford *not* to sow. So, we sowed. Oftentimes our sowing didn't amount to much, but we believed God would cause it to be multiplied and return to us.

As our faith for sowing grew, we could then sow greater sums, which we also believed would multiply. One of the Bible verses we stood on was 2 Corinthians 9:10: *"Now may He who supplies seed to the sower, and bread for food, supply and multiply the seed you have sown and increase the fruits of your righteousness."*

Not only does God *always* provide seed, but He also multiplies that seed. The principle of multiplication runs throughout the Bible. What cannot be achieved by addition, God achieves by multiplication.

A seed in a farmer's pocket accomplishes nothing. Only when it is sown can God multiply it. The same is true for believers. It isn't until we sow our seed that we have the right to believe for maximum results and the highest level attainable. That's why I regularly pray, "God, give me more seed for sowing." Notice, I don't pray, "God, give me this or give me that." I pray for more seed, because as a sower I'll always have the promise of a harvest.

Sowers are never without seed. We always have seed in some form that oftentimes doesn't involve money. Sometimes the best seed we can sow is giving someone a smile, a pat on the back, or a kind and loving word. God always multiplies any seed we sow.

HIGHER LEVEL OF FELLOWSHIP WITH GOD AND HIS WORD

We were created by God to live our lives on a much higher level. The highest level attainable in life is living in fellowship with God and His Word. This means we allow God to order our steps and allow His Word to be final authority in all the affairs of life.

When we allow God to direct our steps, He will show us the path of life. The Bible says, "*You will show me the path of life; in Your presence is fullness of joy; at Your right hand are pleasures forevermore*" (Psalm 16:11). When we are on God's path of life, it will lead us to life at its best.

Being on God's path of life doesn't exempt us from hindrances, obstructions, or opposition. I've learned that walking in God's path brings devils out of the woodwork. They're not simply going to roll over and play dead. They will do everything they can to get us to stop rocking the proverbial boat and to turn back to our old way of living.

But when we are living God's way, God promises we will not be alone. Psalm 23:6 says, *"Surely goodness and mercy shall follow me all the days of my life."* The Passion Translation says, *"So why would I fear the future? Only goodness and tender love pursue me all the days of my life."* That's not a bad way to live. I'd call that the highest level attainable!

King David expressed these words of worship to God: *"The fountain of life flows from You to satisfy me"* (Psalm 36:9 TPT). God is not the source of a mediocre existence. He is the source of real life—life at its best.

The Apostle Paul tells us, *"Those who receive [God's] overflowing grace (unmerited favor) ... reign as kings in life through the one Man Jesus Christ (the Messiah, the Anointed One)"* (Romans 5:17 AMPCE).

God is the source of life. From Him springs all that constitutes life. From Him proceeds all that makes up true joy and happiness in life. In Him we live, we move, and we have our being. Everything that makes life real comes from God.

I've heard it said that loving God is the prerequisite for living our best lives. We must never allow the love of things to become our number one pursuit in life. Rather, we must put God first. This is what enables us to experience maximum living—the highest level attainable.

Putting God first always brings abundant life. THE MESSAGE paraphrase of Romans 5:17 says, "*Can you imagine the breathtaking recovery life makes, absolute life, in those who grasp with both hands this wildly extravagant life-gift, this grand setting-everything-right, that the one man Jesus Christ provides?*" The word *extravagant* means "no restraints; beyond the ordinary."

This sounds like the kind of life we should live! If God has already provided it for us, then why settle for anything less? We can make the decision to live at a higher level. We can choose to walk on God's path of life.

The Word of God says, "*Show me Your ways, O LORD; teach me Your paths*" (Psalm 25:4). Getting on the path of life is the result of being taught, of being directed. That's what the Bible is for—to teach us how to get on God's path of life. But the choice to do so is ours.

According to the Bible, the choice between life and death is solely ours. "*I call heaven and earth as witnesses today against you, that I have set before you life and death, blessing and cursing; therefore, choose life, that both you and your descendants may live*" (Deuteronomy 30:19). I find it interesting that in case we aren't sure which choice is correct, we are told to choose life.

We are to choose the life God desires for us—no longer just existing or barely getting by—but experiencing life at its fullest. Life at its best. We must never accept anything less than what Jesus provided for us through His shed blood. But once we've made our choice, we must take care to guard that which we've been given.

To continually enjoy the maximum and highest level attainable, we must do two things. One, be selective about what comes out of our mouths. Two, be selective about who we associate with.

The Bible says, *"Death and life are in the power of the tongue"* (Proverbs 18:21) and *"He who guards his mouth preserves his life"* (Proverbs 13:3). The Amplified Bible, Classic Edition says, *"He who guards his mouth keeps his life* and The Passion Translation says, *Guard your words, and you'll guard your life."*

Our words matter. I can't stress this truth enough. **Oftentimes people fail to receive God's best simply due to what comes out of their mouths**. They may say, "The economy is rough. I'll probably get laid off at work," or "My grandmother and my mother both died in their fifties, and I probably will too," or "I know we're in time of God's maximum, but it probably won't happen for me." Such individuals have unknowingly become their own worst enemies.

Not only must we guard our mouths, but we must also be selective about who we associate with. Not everyone sees what we see. Not everyone believes what we believe. Not everyone will accept our dreams and encourage us to attain them. Therefore, our friends and those we run with must be people of like precious faith.

My best friends are people who believe for maximum results. They believe for the highest level attainable. But not all the people I encounter share this level of faith. Sometimes they are filled with doubt and unbelief. That's when I put a smile on my face, look them in the eye, and never hear another word they say.

I can be friendly and courteous to such people while at the same time thinking, *That may be what you believe but it's not what I believe. I believe for the maximum results. I'm going for the highest level attainable.* My prayer for those is always, "Bless them Lord. Help them understand. Give them insight and revelation."

Don't run with people who are content to stay as they are. Why would anyone be satisfied in that place when the Bible says there's so much more to attain?

LAUNCH OUT INTO THE DEEP

We are familiar with the story about Jesus teaching the multitudes from Simon (Peter)'s boat, and then afterward telling him to "'*Launch out into the deep and let down your nets for a catch*'" (Luke 5:4). Why did Jesus tell Peter to launch into the deep? Because that's where the maximum catch was.

The Bible tells us that *"Those who go down to the seas in ships, who do business on great waters, they see the works of the LORD, and His wonders in the deep"* (Psalm 107:23–24). The Passion Translation says, *"We saw breathtaking wonders upon the high seas"* and THE MESSAGE paraphrase says, *Out at sea you saw God in action, saw his breathtaking ways with the ocean.*

Those who are willing to get out of the boat, to get off the shores of life, are the people who will see the works and wonders of the Lord. Remaining on the shore prevents believers from experiencing the highest level attainable.

Doing what we are capable of in our own strength will not enable us to receive the maximum, nor will sowing only what we think we can afford. We must be willing to step out of our comfort zones if we want the maximum, the highest attainable level of living.

Comfort zones are areas from which people seldom stray, making their world very small. The Bible says, *"The world of the generous gets larger and larger; the world of the stingy gets smaller and smaller"* (Proverbs 11:24 MSG). The New King James Version says, *"There is one who scatters, yet increases more; and there is one who withholds more than is right, but it leads to poverty"* (Proverbs 11:24).

In other words, when someone stays in his or her comfort zone, withholding instead of sowing, they are headed toward poverty. But let's read the very next verse: *"The generous soul will be made rich, and he who waters will also be watered himself"* (verse 25). Here's the bottom line: When we constantly withhold when we should be giving, our world will become smaller and smaller. But when we sow generously, our world gets larger and larger.

My world today is far larger than when I first started walking in God's path of life. I'm so very grateful for all God has done and all He's blessed me with—both personally and in our ministry. I never dreamed when I came to the Lord in 1969 that this ministry would one day be known around the world. My books and resources have gone to nations I've never been to. The reason is that I've been a faithful sower—both at times when I had little and when I had much.

I never tell people to give away their houses or their cars. But regardless of a person's financial standing, there is always *something* to give. There was a time when I didn't have money to give so I mowed my neighbor's yard. I didn't have money, but I had a lawnmower.

Consistency in giving is the key to increase. Those who refuse to give, when they know they should, not only limit themselves, but they also limit God. Sowing is God's way of our entering into the maximum. It's God's way for us to experience the highest level attainable.

Let's see what the Word of God has to say about the one who deals graciously with others.

> *5A good man sheweth favour, and lendeth: he will guide his affairs with discretion. 6Surely he shall not be moved for ever: the righteous shall be in everlasting remembrance. 7He shall not be afraid of evil tidings: his heart is fixed, trusting in the LORD. 8His heart is established, he shall not be afraid, until he see `righteousness endureth for ever; his horn shall be exalted with honour.* (Psalm 112:5–9 KJV)

This man shows favor to others. He lends, disperses, and gives to the poor. The Passion Translation says, *"Life is good for the one who is generous and charitable... They will not live in fear or dread of what may come... Never stingy and always generous to those in need, they lived lives of influence and honor that will never be forgotten."*

It sounds to me that this person lives to give. God will always have something better for a giver.

CHAPTER 5

TIME TO BREAK LOOSE

Many of us can recall the moment in our walk of faith when we realized we were no longer satisfied living below our privileges as children of God. Some reading this book have also come to that realization. If this is where you are right now, then it's time for you to tap into your dominion and break loose!

This principal of breaking loose begins in the book of Genesis. Isaac was old and knew his days on earth were coming to an end, so he blessed his son Jacob. Then, Jacob's twin brother, Esau, asked his father to bless him too. Here is what happened:

> *39And Isaac his father answered and said unto him, Behold, thy dwelling shall be the fatness of the earth, and of the dew of*

> *heaven from above;* ⁴⁰*And by thy sword shalt thou live, and shalt serve thy brother; and it shall come to pass when thou shalt have the dominion, that thou shalt break his yoke from off thy neck.* (Genesis 27:39–40 KJV)

Isaac decreed that Esau would one day *break loose* from the yoke on his neck. But notice what would precipitate that action. The Amplified Bible, Classic Edition, gives additional insight, saying, *But [the time shall come] when you will grow **restive** and break loose, and you shall take his yoke from off your neck* (verse 40). The word *restive* means "impatient of control; restless; uneasy; dissatisfied."

When believers do not routinely experience the fulfillment of God's promises in their lives, they need to become *restive*. In other words, they need to **get fed up**!

Imagine with me a seventeen-year-old, 6'5", 225-pound high school football tackle about to make the all-state team. His little 4'9" mama walks into his bedroom and says, "Boy, didn't I tell you to clean up your room?"

He says, "Yes, Mama, I'll do it as soon as I can."

She comes back later, and the room is still a mess. "Son, I told you to clean up your bedroom."

"Yes, Mama, I'll do it."

She comes back again, and the room looks just the same. This time she grabs him by the ear, forces him to look her in the eye, and says, "Time is up! You are going to clean your room *now*. If it isn't clean when I get back, you and I are going to go round and round—and I'm telling you right now I will win!" That room got cleaned up. Why? Because Mama got fed up!

Are you fed up with the devil stealing your harvest? Then get fed up and break loose from that situation. The harvest belongs to you! The Word of God says the wealth of the wicked is laid up for the just. Another way the Bible says it is *"the wealth of the sinner [finds its way eventually] into the hands of the righteous, for whom it was laid up"* (Proverbs 13:22 AMPCE).

When is eventually? When you get fed up with your harvest being in the wrong hands. When you get restive and are no longer willing to live beneath your privileges as a child of God. You must reach the place where you are restive, fed up, and no longer willing to live without the privileges that are yours as a child of God.

God wants us to experience His maximum. To fully experience all that He has for us, we must not only break loose from the enemy's yoke of bondage, but we must also be obedient to follow God's instructions. Let's look at what happened when God's people allowed their personal issues to keep them from following His instructions.

> [1]*In the second year of King Darius, in the sixth month, on the first day of the month, the word of the LORD came by Haggai the prophet ...* [2]*"Thus speaks the LORD of hosts, saying 'This people says, "The time has not come, the time that the LORD's house should be built." ' "*
>
> [3]*Then the word of the LORD came by Haggai the prophet, saying,* [4]*"Is it time for you yourselves to dwell in your paneled houses, and this temple to lie in ruins?"*

> *⁵Now therefore, thus says the LORD of hosts: "Consider your ways! ⁶You have sown much, and bring in little; you eat, but do not have enough; you drink, but you are not filled with drink; you clothe yourselves, but no one is warm; and he who earns wages, earns wages to put into a bag with holes."*
>
> *⁷Thus says the LORD of hosts: "Consider your ways!"* (Haggai 1:1–7)

If the promises of God are not being fulfilled in our lives, instead of questioning God we must question our ways.

CONSIDER YOUR WAYS

The Bible says, *"There is a way that seems right to a man, but its end is the way of death"* (Proverbs 14:12 and Proverbs 16:25). This truth is so important that it appears verbatim *twice* in the book of Proverbs.

But here's the good news: God's way is *always* right, *all* the time. All we need to do is find God's way of doing things, and then do it.

Let's look again at the word God spoke through Haggai: *You have sown much, and bring in little* (verse 6). That scenario is in direct violation of spiritual law. Those who sow much are entitled to reap much according to the Word of God: *[Remember]this: he who sows sparingly and grudgingly will also reap sparingly and grudgingly, and he who sows generously [that blessings may come to someone] will also reap generously and with blessings* (2 Corinthians 9:6 AMPCE).

Through Haggai, the Lord also addressed those who do not have enough to eat and drink, insufficient clothing, and lack in wages. And then He says again, "Consider your ways!" God doesn't need to say anything but once, but when He says something twice, we need to pay close attention. He is trying to help us, not condemn us. He wants us to get maximum results and attain the highest level. Doing so requires that we put God and His Word first in our lives.

In what is known as Jesus' Sermon on the Mount, He tells the people they cannot serve God and mammon. Then He lovingly asks a series of questions that allows those present to consider their ways.

> [25]*"Therefore I say to you, do not worry about your life, what you will eat or what you will drink; nor about your body, what you will put on. Is not life more than food and the body more than clothing?* [26]*Look at the birds of the air, for they neither sow nor reap nor gather into barns; yet your heavenly Father feeds them. Are you not of more value than they?* [27]*Which of you by worrying can add one cubit to his stature?*
>
> [28]*So why do you worry about clothing? Consider the lilies of the field, how they grow: they neither toil nor spin;* [29]*and yet I say to you that even Solomon in all His glory was not arrayed like one of these.* [30]*Now if God so clothes the grass of the field, which today is, and tomorrow is thrown into the oven, will*

*He not much more clothe you, O you of little
faith?"*

³¹*"Therefore do not worry, saying, 'What
shall we eat?' or 'What shall we drink?'
or 'What shall we wear?' ³²For after these
things the Gentiles seek. For your heavenly
Father knows that you need all these things."*
(Matthew 6:25–32)

Jesus led the crowd to consider their ways. But then He
gave them the key to *God's way* of doing things. He said, "*But
seek **first** the kingdom of God and His righteousness, and all
these things shall be added to you*" (Matthew 6:33). These
words are as powerful and true for us as when they were first
spoken. Jesus is establishing for us *correct priorities.*

In essence, He says, "Don't be like the Gentiles who
purse these things. Rather, purse Me first and all these things
will be added. Don't be like everybody else. Dare to be
different."

The Amplified Bible, Classic Edition, translation of
Matthew 6:33 says, "*But seek (aim at and strive after) first
of all His kingdom and His righteousness (His way of doing
and being right), and then all these things taken together
will be given you besides.*"

GOD'S WAYS ALWAYS WORK

The Bible makes this powerful statement: "*The fear of
the LORD is the beginning of knowledge, but fools despise
wisdom and instruction*" (Proverbs 1:7). The fool is right in
his own thinking. That's the reason he's a fool.

But we are not fools—*if* we choose to seek first the kingdom of God, His righteousness, and His ways. Any time we are headed the wrong direction, our heavenly Father will correct us. All we have to do is *receive* His correction, for the Bible says, "*A fool despises his father's instruction, but he who receives correction is prudent*" (Proverbs 15:5).

When we seek God's way of doing things, we don't need a "plan B." THE MESSAGE paraphrase says, "*People who don't know God and the way He works fuss over these things, but you both know God and how He works ... Don't worry about missing out*" (Matthew 6:32-33). By putting God—and His Word and His ways—first, we won't miss out on anything!

The Bible gives us the correct priorities. When we focus on God's Word and His way of doing things instead of the things we want, then all the "things" will be added to us. Psalm 34:10 says, "*But those who seek the LORD shall not lack any good thing.*" The Bible also says, *Blessed (happy, fortunate, to be envied) are they who keep His testimonies, and who seek, inquire for and of Him and crave Him with the whole heart*" (Psalm 119:2 AMPCE).

The word *blessed* means "empowered to prosper; to excel; to rise above what holds others down." When we put God's Word and His kingdom in first place, then all kinds of blessings come our way. Not only prosperity and material blessings, but also the favor of God.

God spoke these words through the prophet Isaiah: "'*For My thoughts are not your thoughts, nor are your ways My ways*'" (Isaiah 55:8). He made it clear that the way mankind thinks and the way He thinks are different. They are not in agreement. He goes on to say, "'*For as the heavens are*

*higher than the earth, so are My ways higher than your ways,
and My thoughts than your thoughts'"* (verse 9).

Now let's look at verse 11. God says, *"'So shall My
word be that goes forth from My mouth; it shall not return to
Me void, but it shall accomplish what I please, and it shall
prosper in the thing for which I sent it.'"*

My point is this: God's thoughts and ways are higher
than ours. God's Word (His way) is always right. We need
to stop telling God how to do things, and instead seek His
way of doing things and being right. The Bible says, *Trust
in the LORD with all your heart, and lean not on your own
understanding. In all your ways acknowledge Him, and He
shall direct your paths* (Proverbs 3:5–6).

God *wants* to show us His ways. It is utterly foolish for
us to attempt to get God to think like we do or do things our
way. God wants us to experience His best in every area of
life. He wants us to experience maximum results and the
highest attainable level of living. Doing things His way is
the *only* way that is going to take place.

POSITIONED TO RECEIVE GOD'S BEST

The Apostle Paul revealed that when we make Jesus the
Lord of our lives, we become new creations. Old things are
passed away and all things become new (see 2 Corinthians
5:17). We receive the very nature of God when we are
born again.

According to 1 Corinthians 2:16, we have the *"mind of
Christ."* This means we can think those higher thoughts that
God thinks and do things on a higher level. In other words,
we are positioned to receive God's best.

Paul also tells us that as we continue this process of renewing the mind, we will be put in *that good and acceptable and perfect will of God* (Romans 12:2). I personally believe that when we are in the perfect will of God, we are positioned to receive His best. Yet we have a part to play in receiving all God has for us.

That part is to exercise our faith, for the Word of God says, *"Now faith is the substance of things hoped for, the evidence of things not seen"* (Hebrews 11:1). And that faith must be activated by love. The Amplified Bible, Classic Edition, says it like this: *"only faith activated and energized and expressed and working through love [counts]"* (brackets added).

Many in the body of Christ miss God's best because they do not operate in faith and love. Jesus said, *"By this all will know that you are My disciples, if you have love for one another"* (John 13:35).

Years ago, a certain preacher made a point to criticize me for preaching the Word of Faith message. Then, only two weeks later, I received a letter from him asking for money to help make a needed purchase for his church. I thought, *He doesn't want to hear the message of faith, but he sure does want what it will produce!*

I could have written back and said, "I heard you talking ugly about me. You're on your own buddy!" But I didn't. Instead, I started to tear the letter in half before throwing it in the trash. But the Lord stopped me.

He said, "What are you going to do about that preacher's request?"

"Nothing," I answered.

"Send him some money."

"Lord, why would I want to send him anything? He criticized me."

"What does my Word say about walking in love?"

At that moment I wanted to ask the Lord if He didn't have something better to do than continue the conversation. But He had made His point. His thoughts and ways were higher than my thoughts and ways. If I wanted God's best, then I had to walk in the kind of faith that is activated and brought to perfection by love.

Hebrews 11:6 tells us that without faith, it is impossible to please God. The Apostle Paul declared that *"The just shall live by faith"* (Romans 1:17), and Jesus commanded His disciples to *"Have faith in God"* (Mark 11:22). To *live by faith* means to have our lives sustained—maintained, upheld, supported—by faith. The kind of faith that pleases God is the life of faith that expresses complete and total trust in Him and in His Word.

In the ninth chapter of Matthew is the story of a paralytic man being lowered by his friends through the roof into a room where Jesus was preaching. The Bible says, *When Jesus saw their faith, He said to the paralytic, "Son, be of good cheer; your sins are forgiven you"* (verse 2). According to this story, faith can be seen.

When God sees our faith as an expression of compete trust in Him, then, according to Jesus, *"Nothing will be impossible for you"* (Matthew 17:20).

Experiencing maximum results and reaching the highest level attainable may sound impossible. But when you have faith that is motivated by love, it is not impossible.

DON'T FALL INTO THE ENEMY'S TRAP

In Paul's second letter to Timothy, whom he referred to as his son in the faith, he told the young man how to avoid falling into the enemy's trap.

> *Flee also youthful lusts; but pursue righteousness, faith, love, peace with those who call on the Lord out of a pure heart. But avoid foolish and ignorant disputes, knowing that they generate strife. And a servant of the Lord must not quarrel but be gentle to all, able to teach, patient, in humility correcting those who are in opposition, if God perhaps will grant them repentance, so that they may know the truth, and that they may come to their senses and escape the snare of the devil, having been taken captive by him to do his will.* (2 Timothy 2:22–26)

I want to focus on two things Paul instructed Timothy to do to avoid the snare of the devil. One: pursue righteousness, faith, love, and peace. Two: avoid strife.

We have already determined that faith works, or is perfected, by love. Without love, our faith never gets perfected. I'm not talking only about loving God, but also loving others—including the unlovely. Jesus said, *"But if you love those who love you, what credit is that to you? For even sinners love those who love them"* (Luke 6:32).

Do not allow the enemy to use someone you have a grudge against to block your blessings. Whatever you perceive that person did to you, they likely are unaware of their words or actions and have never given the matter another thought. He or she has gone on with life, yet you are allowing your feelings for that person to block your blessing.

The Bible says, "*The only thing that counts is faith expressing itself through love*" (Galatians 5:6 NIV). That one sentence from the Bible is a powerful truth, considering the Bible contains sixty-six books, 1,188 chapters, and more than 31,000 verses.

What matters most is faith working through love. Jesus said, "*A new commandment I give to you, that you love one another; as I have loved you, that you also love one another. By this all will know that you are My disciples, if you have love for one another*" (John 13:34–35).

Failure to walk in love is only part of the reason some believers are not walking in God's blessing and all that He wants them to attain. They may argue, "But I have great faith, Brother Jerry." That's wonderful, but do have strife in your life? We just read Paul's words to Timothy: *But avoid foolish and ignorant disputes, knowing that they generate strife* (2 Timothy 2:23).

If you have any strife in your life today, then don't go another minute with it, you must not allow strife in your home. You must not allow strife in your family—get rid of it at any cost. Strife is a blessing blocker! Paul refers to it in his letter to Timothy (II Timothy 2:26) as a "snare of the devil," a trap. It's designed to hold you back. It's designed to keep you from experiencing God's best.

Most of us are familiar with Jesus' teaching in Mark 11, in which He made the vital connection between faith and forgiveness.

[22]So Jesus answered and said to them, "Have faith in God. [23]For assuredly, I say to you, whoever says to this mountain, 'Be removed and be cast into the sea,' and does not doubt in his heart, but believes that those things he says will be done, he will have whatever he says. [24]Therefore I say to you, whatever things you ask when you pray, believe that you receive them, and you will have them. [25]And whenever you stand praying, if you have anything against anyone, forgive him, that your Father in heaven may also forgive you your trespasses." (Mark 11:22–25)

TRUTH IS ANOTHER WORD for FAITH

If we want to attain all God has for us, all that His Word promises us, then we must exercise faith that is empowered by love as we walk in forgiveness toward those who have wronged us. I remember Brother Copeland once saying it this way, "Faith won't work in an unforgiving heart."

Paul wrote to the believers in Ephesus and instructed them to be rooted and grounded in love (see Ephesians 3:17). He also said, *"I, therefore, the prisoner of the Lord, beseech you to walk worthy of the calling with which you were called [2]...bearing with one another in love* (Ephesians 4:1–2). The Amplified Bible, Classic Edition, says *"bearing with one another and making allowances because you love one another."* Love makes allowances. Love does not condemn. Love does not promote itself.

Paul sent this letter of thanks and encouragement that detailed his prayer for all the saints, bishops, and deacons at

Philippi: "*³I thank my God in all my remembrance of you. ⁴In every prayer of mine I always make my entreaty and petition for you all with joy (delight) ... ⁹And this I pray: that your love may abound yet more and more and extend to its fullest development*"(Philippians 1:3–4, 9 AMPCE).

According to Romans 10:17, faith comes by hearing and hearing, meaning we can grow our faith. But Paul tells us that we can also grow our love and become stronger in our love walk. It takes both faith and love—faith working by love—to produce the results we desire. It takes faith to break loose from that which holds us back.

The prophet Isaiah said, *Shake yourself from the dust; arise, sit [erect in a dignified place], O Jerusalem; loose yourself from the bonds of your neck, O captive Daughter of Zion* (Isaiah 52:2). It's time to break loose from all that has prevented us from receiving God's maximum!

CHAPTER 6

PUT FIRST THINGS FIRST

In the previous chapter we read Haggai 1:1–7 in the context of the Lord saying to the people, *"Consider your ways!"* There is yet more for us to learn from the words of Haggai as he stirred the people's hearts to return to their purpose.

The Babylonian empire had destroyed the temple some seventy years earlier. God had given His people the task of rebuilding it, but they kept putting it off. Instead, they built their own good houses and left God's house in ruins.

Though God had given them the assignment to rebuild, they kept saying, "It's not time." They pursued their own desires and wants. God's people suffered for their procrastination and misplaced priorities: they didn't experience the maximum, the highest level attainable. They did not put first things first, and as a result, they were failing in their purpose from God!

Albert E.N. Gray was an official at the Prudential Life Insurance Company of America. It was said that he spent his life searching for the one single trait shared by all successful people. His book, *The Common Denominator of Success,* released in 1940, made a significant impact on me.

According to Gray, successful people's common characteristic was not hard work, though hard work is important. Rather, the number one characteristic was that each had the habit of doing the things failures don't like to do. In other words, putting first things first.

Gray said that successful people also don't like to do these things, but their dislike of doing them is subordinate to the strength of their purpose, which is to fulfill their goals.

The book of Haggai essentially communicates the same message.

> "*2 Thus speaks the LORD of hosts, saying, 'This people says, "The time has not come, the time that the LORD's house should be built." ' " 3Then the word of the LORD came by Haggai the prophet, saying, "4Is it time for you yourselves to dwell in your paneled houses, and this temple to lie in ruins?" 5Now therefore, thus says the LORD of hosts: "Consider your ways!*
>
> "*6You have sown much, and bring in little; you eat, but do not have enough; you drink, but you are not filled with drink; you clothe yourselves, but no one is warm; and he who*

earns wages, earns wages to put into bags with holes."

⁷Thus says the LORD of hosts: "Consider your ways!" (Haggai 1:2–7)

It is never God's ways that prevent us from experiencing His best—it is *our* ways!

God sent Haggai to His people to help get their priorities back in line with what they should have been doing: what was pleasing to God. But they had begun to drift away from God. Their priorities were misplaced.

A lot of Christians are like this today, living with misplaced priorities. They want to succeed. God also wants them to succeed, but it cannot be done by putting the desire for success before seeking God.

In Old Testament times, not only was the fact that the temple was in ruins an indication God's people were prone to procrastination, but it also indicated a neglect in worshipping God. The temple was the place where they worshipped Him. I've learned that when God's people get sloppy in the everyday matters of life, they also get sloppy in their relationship with God. That's what happened in Haggai's day.

THE MESSAGE paraphrase of 1 Corinthians 10:11 says, *"These are all warning markers—DANGER!—in our history books, written down so that we don't repeat their mistakes."* The reason we have this account in the book of Haggai is for our benefit, so that we can avoid their mistakes.

HERE ARE FIVE PRINCIPLES WE CAN TAKE FROM THE BOOK OF HAGGAI:

- To have an advantage
- We must stop making excuses for not putting first things *first*.
- We must stop being selfish, thinking only of our own wants and desires.
- We must take a good look at where we've put the things of God on our list of priorities.
- We must stop being the reason that our blessings are blocked.
- We must place God in the *highest* position in our lives, now and forever.

PUT GOD FIRST

When God revealed His Ten Commandments to Moses on Mount Sinai, He said, *"I am the LORD your God, who brought you out of the land of Egypt, out of the house of bondage"* (Exodus 20:2). And then He gave the first commandment: *"You shall have no other gods before Me"* (verse 3).

Moses later reviewed the commandments with the people of Israel, saying, *"You shall love the LORD your God with all your heart, with all your soul, and with all your strength"* Deuteronomy 6:5. THE MESSAGE paraphrase says, *Love GOD, your God, with your whole heart: love Him with all that's in you, love Him with all you've got!*

Our greatest love and our deepest affection should be directed to God, who spoke these words to Abraham, *"I am the Almighty God; walk and live habitually before Me and be perfect (blameless, wholehearted, complete)"* (Genesis 17:1 AMPCE). The word *habitually* means "unending; unceasing; not seasonal." We could also add, not only when everything is going well.

Jesus made this statement: *"If you love Me, keep My commandments"* (John 14:15). THE MESSAGE paraphrase says, *"If you love me, show it by doing what I've told you."* In other words, Jesus was saying, "I want more than just words. I appreciate you saying that you love Me, but I want you to show Me by doing what I've told you to do."

One of the major things Jesus told us we are to do is found in Matthew 6:33, *"But seek ye first the kingdom of God and His righteousness..."* (KJV). The word *first* means "in the foremost place; the highest or greatest of importance; ranking above all else; prominent."

The Amplified Bible, Classic Edition, says *"But seek (aim at and strive after) first of all His kingdom and His righteousness (His way of doing and being right)."* Jesus wants us to follow *His* way of doing and being right. If we're going to do this, then we obviously need to spend some time in the Word of God to learn His way of doing things. The best place to start is the beginning.

> *Then God said, "Let Us make man in Our image, according to Our likeness; let them have dominion over the fish of the sea, over the birds of the air, and over the cattle, over all the earth and over every creeping thing*

that creeps on the earth." So God created man in His own image; in the image of God He created him; male and female He created them. Then God blessed them, and God said to them, "Be fruitful and multiply; fill the earth and subdue it; have dominion over the fish of the sea, over the birds of the air, and over every living thing that moves on the earth." (Genesis 1:26–28)

Notice God *blessed* them with five specific blessings: (1) be fruitful, (2) multiply, (3) fill the earth, (4) subdue it, and (5) have dominion. This fivefold blessing shows us it was God's intention from the beginning that mankind experience His maximum blessing and walk perpetually in the highest level of life attainable on earth.

But how were they do so? We find the answer in the next verse: *"And God said, 'See, I have given you every herb that yields seed which is on the face of all the earth, and every tree whose fruit yields seed; to you it shall be for food'"* (Genesis 1:29).

God empowered mankind to prosper by blessing them. The word *blessed* means "empowered to prosper." In other words, God was saying, "Now that I've empowered you to prosper, go be successful. Use the seed I've given you for your provision." From the beginning, sowing seed has been God's way for mankind to have provision—not only for the food we eat, but for every other need we have. Seed is for *provision.*

God intended that we sustain our lives through the seeds we sow. This was true in the beginning, and it remains true today. We know, of course, that God will bless the works of our hands. That's part of being successful and living well. However, God doesn't want us to depend solely on what we can do alone with our own hands. God gets involved with our works when we sow seed. That's how we link ourselves with the supernatural.

Now let me speak personally to you. What are your greatest needs and desires at this moment? Take the time to write them on a piece of paper or make a list on your computer. Once you do so, think about what you can sow toward seeing your needs and desires fulfilled. God is interested in your needs and desires. He's the God who cares.

I want to share something I learned to do years ago. When I receive a prophetic word, the first thing I do is write it down. The next thing I do is have it printed for my notebook. The Bible says, *"Write the vision and make it plain on tablets"* (Habakkuk 2:2). In other words, keep the vision before you so that it will motivate you. The next thing I do is think and pray about the seed I will sow to ensure the prophetic word comes to pass in my life. And then I sow it.

I continue to do what God told Adam to do in the beginning: sow seed. God also made this promise: *"While the earth remains, seedtime and harvest ... shall not cease"* (Genesis 8:22). This means that if we continue to practice God's way of doing things—sowing and reaping—then we can expect His kind of results.

Jesus made this statement: *"Behold, a sower went out to sow"* (Matthew 13:3). That's what sowers do. Sowing should be as natural to sowers as breathing. The Bible says, *"Do not be deceived, God is not mocked; for whatever a man sows, that he will also reap"* (Galatians 6:7). The Passion

77

Translation says, *"God will not be mocked! For what you plant will always be the very thing you harvest."*

So, who is in charge of the harvest? We are. We determine the kind of harvest we will receive.

When we sow seed, we should *expect* a harvest. No farmer goes to a field and says, "This is a waste of time. I'm not going to sow, but I still expect a harvest" or "Give me a harvest and then I'll plant some seed." There is no harvest without *first* sowing seed! We put first things first when we sow seed.

The Bible makes this promise: *"And let us not grow weary while doing good, for in due season we shall reap if we do not lose heart"* (Galatians 6:9). The *well doing* Paul refers to in this verse is sowing. That's the theme of Galatians 6. THE MESSAGE paraphrase says, *"At the right time we will harvest a good crop if we don't give up, or quit."* The Passion Translation says, *for the season of reaping the wonderful harvest you've planted is coming!"* The harvest is coming!

SEED IS FOR PROVISION

We learned in the previous section that the seed God gives us is for the purpose of provision, to sustain us. Let's see how this eternal law of *seedtime and harvest* for the purpose of provision manifested in a familiar story from the Old Testament. At the time, there had been no rain for years, and the land experienced famine. That's when the Lord spoke to the prophet Elijah.

⁸And the word of the LORD came unto him, saying, ⁹Arise, get thee to Zarephath, which belongeth to Zidon, and dwell there: behold, I have commanded a widow woman there to sustain thee. ¹⁰So he arose and went to Zarephath. And when he came to the gate of the city, behold, the widow woman was there gathering of sticks: and he called to her, and said, Fetch me, I pray thee, a little water in a vessel, that I may drink.

¹¹And as she was going to fetch it, he called to her, and said, Bring me, I pray thee, a morsel of bread in thine hand. ¹²And she said, As the LORD thy God liveth, I have not a cake, but a handful of meal in a barrel, and a little oil in a cruse: and, behold, I am gathering two sticks, that I may go in and dress it for me and my son, that we may eat it, and die. (1 Kings 17: 8–12 KJV)

Notice in verse 9 the words "sustain thee." The woman was going to do something for Elijah that would sustain him, but her obedience to the word of the Lord through the prophet would also sustain her, as we will see.

> *¹³And Elijah said to her, Fear not; go and do as thou hast said: but make me thereof a little cake first, and bring it unto me, and after make for thee and for thy son. ¹⁴For thus saith the LORD God of Israel, The barrel of meal shall not waste, neither shall the cruse of oil fail, until the day that the LORD sendeth rain upon the earth.*
>
> *¹⁵And she went and did according to the saying of Elijah: and she, and he, and*

> *her house, did eat for many days. ¹⁶And*
> *the barrel of meal wasted not, neither did*
> *the cruse of oil fail, according to the word*
> *of the LORD, which he spake by Elijah.*
> (1 Kings 17:13–16 KJV)

The words *she went and did* may be the most important words in this story. What did she do? She first made Elijah a little cake. What we do first matters to God. What we do first determines whether we experience the maximum and the highest level attainable. That woman's willingness to obey opened the door for her to experience the supernatural.

My greatest harvests have been the result of my sowing when the conditions weren't perfect. The Bible says, *"He who observes the wind [and waits for all conditions to be favorable] will not sow, and he who regards the clouds will not reap"* (Ecclesiastes 11:4 AMPCE). It's easy to sow when conditions are perfect, but it takes faith to sow when, in the natural, it doesn't look like a good time to sow.

If we wait for perfect conditions before we sow, Satan will see to it that the conditions are never perfect.

At the beginning of this chapter, we read the words Haggai spoke to the people who'd let God's house sit in ruins. He said to them twice, "Consider your ways!" So, what happened? The Bible says, *"So the LORD stirred up ... the spirit of all the remnant of the people; and they came and worked on the house of the LORD of hosts, their God"* (Haggai 1:14). And then the Lord said, *"... But from this day I will bless you"* (Haggai 2:19).

Just as when the widow put first things first and fed the prophet, and was blessed by God, so the people finally put first things first and heard God say, "From this day I will bless you."

When we choose to put first things first according to God's Word, God will take us to the maximum, the highest level attainable, in the name of Jesus!

CHAPTER 7

GIVING QUALIFIES US FOR GOD'S MAXIMUM

I refuse to own anything that I'm not willing to give away. That's a bold statement, but it's one I've proven to the Lord many *times* over the years. I've given away cars. I've given away motorcycles. I've given away airplanes. I've had people bless me with brand new suits that I never wore because the Lord said, *"Now you have something you can give that preacher who needs it."*

I learned that any time I sow a seed that was first sown into my life in ministry, it becomes a twice-sown seed.

Carolyn and I live to give. It's the reason we are so blessed today. We don't approach giving as a one-time event. It's our lifestyle. This is the basis on which we stand for God's maximum, the hundredfold return, in our lives. Again, Jesus said there are none who, when He asks them to give for His sake and the Gospel's, that shall not receive a hundredfold now in this time (see Mark 10:30).

God doesn't ask us to give something and not expect a return on the seed we sow. Some have said, "Well, Brother Jerry, I know people who haven't received a return on their giving." No, you know people who haven't stood in faith for their return. They gave up on it.

Those of us who preach the Word of God concerning prosperity have many critics. I'm always amazed when a preacher will stand up and proclaim to his congregation that he doesn't believe in the prosperity message, and then receive an offering. That's being double minded.

Prosperity is the fuel of God's kingdom. It's how we do the things we need to do to advance His kingdom. The Bible says, *"Let the LORD be magnified, Who has pleasure in the prosperity of His servant"* (Psalm 35:27). We can't help to build the kingdom if we aren't prospering. We can't significantly support missions if we aren't prospering.

According to the Word of God, prosperity is part of our inheritance. Jesus went to the cross that we might be redeemed. And one of the things He redeemed us from was poverty. The Bible says, *"Beloved, I pray that you may prosper in all things and be in health, just as your soul prospers"* (3 John 2). When we are in health and prospering, we are useful to the kingdom of God.

In chapter 1 we studied the story of Jesus and the rich young ruler, who asked Him what he must do to inherit eternal life. Jesus said, *"Go your way, sell whatever you have and give to the poor ... and come, take up the cross, and follow Me"* (Mark 10:21). But the cost seemed too high, and the man walked away.

It was at this point in the narrative that Jesus revealed this truth to His disciples: those who are willing to surrender their lives fully and completely will eventually receive back far more than they were willing to give. *"Assuredly, I say to you, there is no one who has left house or brothers or sisters or father or mother or wife or children or lands, for My sake and the Gospel's, who shall not receive a hundredfold now in this time"* (Mark 10:29–30).

We could say the theme of this story is "the gain of giving all." In other words, if we're willing to make the commitment that everything we have is at God's disposal, then Jesus assures us that anything we give away, we will receive back a hundredfold, or the maximum.

Giving just once doesn't entitle anyone to receiving the maximum. It takes a lifestyle of this kind of giving, a commitment to following Jesus.

Jesus said to His disciples, *"It is easier for a camel to go through the eyes of a needle than for a rich man to enter the kingdom of God"* (Mark 10:25). Peter responded, saying, *"See, we have left all and followed You"* (verse 28). Peter and the others had made a deep, lifetime commitment to follow Jesus. They'd walked away from everything.

Now, God doesn't ask everyone to make this kind of commitment, but He does require it of some. Abraham had to do it. When I made Jesus Lord of my life in 1969, He didn't say, "I want you to leave Carolyn and your daughters and come follow Me." He didn't ask me to walk away from my family. He didn't tell me to leave my house or give up my business (though I did make that decision about my business on my own). He didn't ask me to get rid of my hot rods or the things I enjoyed. I also did that on my own.

I said, "Lord, I want You to know that You are now number one in my life. I've been living *my* dream for my life for many years, but now I want to live *Your* dream for my life. I want to do what You desire me to do, and I'm willing to walk away from my dream to do it."

In the early days of my walk with the Lord, I heard from countless religious-minded people who couldn't resist telling me all the things I had to do to please God, and all the things I could do that would displease Him.

I remember one Sunday morning before church thinking I had just enough time to change out the rear-end of a car I was working on before it was time to leave. From the time I was a little boy working on cars with my dad, he'd drilled these words into my head: "Son, don't ever get under a car without first putting jack stands under it." (A jack raises a vehicle; the jack stand holds the vehicle in place). But I was in a hurry, so I raised the vehicle with a floor jack, scooted my upper body beneath it, and removed both rear wheels. That's when I saw the jack begin to collapse. The car was coming down on me.

The next thing I knew, I was standing a few feet from the vehicle looking at it on the ground. Had I been beneath it I would have been crushed. I believe God caused my angel to pull me to safety because there is no way I could have moved fast enough in my own strength.

At church later that morning, thinking the experience was a great testimony, I made the mistake of telling someone what had happened. I couldn't believe what they said to me. "You shouldn't have been working on a car when it was time to go to church. God was trying to teach you a lesson!" God doesn't harm people to teach them a lesson. Jesus said, *"The thief does not come except to steal, and to kill, and to destroy. I have come that they may have life, and that they may have it more abundantly"* (John 10:10).

Another time, while Carolyn and I were attending a Kenneth Copeland meeting, our girls were being cared for in the nursery. Terri crawled behind a rocking chair, and two of her fingertips were accidently cut off. The surgeon who treated her said it was impossible for them to ever be normal again. She would never have nails. But he did a skin graft and repaired them as best he could.

Carolyn and I refused to agree with what the surgeon told us. We believed God would heal Terri's fingers.

One day, some folks who attended church with us came over to the house to comfort us. One of the women said, "We just don't know why God would cut your baby's fingers off." I was still a new believer at that time, and all I wanted to do was smack her. The best I could do was let them know it was time for them to leave our house.

God didn't cut our baby's fingers off, and Carolyn and I wouldn't allow such talk in our house. I made more than a few people mad, but I was not going to tolerate unbelief and religious tradition.

Several weeks later when we took Terri back to the surgeon's office and he removed the dressing, he stepped back and shouted, "My God!" Terri's fingertips were completely restored, and she had the two most beautiful little fingernails on them.

My Bible tells me the Holy Ghost is our teacher. If car accidents, sickness, and disease were teaching tools, then the devil would be our teacher—and he is not! Speaking of the Holy Ghost, Jesus said, *"However, when He, the Spirit of truth, has come, He will guide you into all truth"* (John16:13).

There are times when we need to turn a proverbial deaf ear to some people. And I'm talking about some Christians.

A LIFELONG COMMITMENT

To experience God's best always requires an unwavering, lifelong commitment to Him and His Word. Commitment involves obedience, determination, focus, and discipline.

Many Christians don't like the word *discipline.* It takes discipline to walk with Jesus. Without discipline, there would be no disciples—then or now. I believe we are living in the last days. I also believe it is the *Word of Faith* that will reach the masses in these times. Why? Because it works! People are realizing that their religious tradition can't help them. It's going to take the uncompromising Word of God to guide us safely through all the chaos and turmoil in the world.

It takes discipline to excel at anything, and that includes a life of faith. Discipline allows us to say, "I'm not moved by what I see. I'm not moved by what I hear. I'm not moved by what I feel. I'm moved only by what I believe. And I believe the Word of God!" It takes discipline to say, "I'm willing to leave all" and then do it.

Committed people are entitled to God's maximum, the highest level attainable. It's only the commitments we make with our whole heart that cause us to receive all God desires for us to have and enjoy.

I made a commitment to Carolyn on July 15, 1966, and I've honored that commitment. There's never been another woman in my life. We haven't fallen out of love with each other, and we are enjoying the fruits of that commitment to each other and to God.

I also made a commitment to God. I said, "There will be no other gods before You." I've kept and honored that commitment, and God has kept His word to me. I'm now experiencing more of His blessings than I ever have, and I'm headed for the maximum, and the highest level attainable. Yes, and the best is yet to come!

It is vital that we remain focused on the commitments we make because we have an enemy who will always attempt to distract us. I've learned that one of the ways to identify when we're on the threshold of a breakthrough is when Satan throws something at us to distract us. He knows that if we remain focused on our commitment, it's just a matter of time before we receive God's best.

Staying committed involves enduring hardship from time to time. There are times when we will be tempted to quit. To give up. To back down and say, "It's just not worth it." That's Satan's way of trying to get us out of position to experience God's best.

Following the Lord and obeying His Word is the most rewarding commitment we will ever make. That's what Jesus endeavored to tell His disciples in the tenth chapter of Mark when He said they would receive a hundredfold, the maximum and highest level attainable.

The maximum belongs to committed believers. The highest level belongs to committed believers.

Right now, ask yourself these questions:
- Am I a committed believer?
- Do I love God above all else?
- Is everything I own available to God?

God has blessed me with some things that I've really enjoyed. But He's also asked me to give some of those things to someone else. That's when I demonstrate that He is still number one in my life.

In 1975, God blessed this ministry with its first debt-free airplane. God proved to me that He could do what men said couldn't be done. I was one happy camper.

The day it arrived we put it in the hangar. The plan was to fly it to St. Simons Island, Georgia, the next morning. As I was shutting the hangar door a question came to my mind. *What if God asks me to give it away before I ever fly it?* I locked the hangar door, got in the car with Carolyn and the girls, and we headed home. But a few minutes later I said, "Carolyn, we have to go back."

"Why?" she asked.

"Well, I've got to do something," I said.

So, I drove back to the airport, opened the hangar door, and then we all laid our hands on that airplane. I prayed, "God, if we never get to fly this then I want you to know that it was a joy watching You do the impossible. If You tell me to give it away before tomorrow, I will do it without reservation and without hesitation."

I'll never forget what He said: "*I commend you for that, Son. Now go enjoy your airplane for now.*"

I enjoyed that plane for nearly two years. At the time, two minister friends of mine were both going through some trying financial challenges. The Lord said, "*I want you to sell the airplane and divide the money between those two ministers. That money will save both ministries.*"

I did as the Lord instructed and sold the airplane to a broker at Meacham Field. Then I gave the money to the two ministers. Immediately I heard the devil say, "What are you going to do now?"

I said, "Well, I'll do what I did before I got the airplane. I'll either drive or fly commercial."

Back then DFW didn't exist. Anyone living in the Dallas-Fort Worth area flew out of Love Field, which was now a hardship on me. I'd set up my preaching schedule based on owning an airplane, and commercial flight schedules weren't always convenient.

I did what had to be done to keep my meeting commitments, and I never had to cancel even one. I never had to break my word to anyone. All the time, we were believing God for our next debt-free airplane. That plane didn't come overnight, but we held fast to the Word of God until it did come. And that was ten debt-free airplanes ago.

I recall the time I was preaching in a meeting with Happy Caldwell, Buddy Harrison, and Ed Dufresne. Ed had just gone through a difficult time in his life and was still hurting. As I listened to him preach that night, the Lord spoke to me. "*Ed doesn't think I hear his prayers because he is hurting. I want you to give him your airplane.*"

At the time I was flying a Cessna 421 Golden Eagle. We'd flown it to the meeting. I'd just overhauled both engines, installed new avionics, redone the interior, and given it a fresh paint job. I had only twenty hours on that plane—it was like new.

91

So, I turned to Carolyn and said, "The Lord just told me to give Ed the airplane."

She said, "I know you. You'll obey God."

As Ed continued to preach, I asked the Lord, "Do you want me to do this publicly or privately?"

He said, "*Just hold on. I'll arrange everything.*"

It wasn't more than fifteen seconds later that Ed abruptly stopped preaching. He looked at me and said, "Jerry, God just told you to do something. Obey him." Ed later told me he thought God spoke to me about someone in the meeting whom He wanted to heal.

So, when Ed called on me, I said to the Lord, "Apparently You want me to do this publicly."

I walked to the platform and, with all eyes on me and Ed, I said, "Ed, I know you're hurting, and God knows you're hurting. You've even said to yourself, 'I wonder if God really hears my prayers.' Ed, God just told me to give you my airplane."

Ed was overwhelmed. He'd been believing for an airplane. God had given me that airplane, and now I was giving it to Ed. The point of the story is this: If that airplane had me instead of me having it, I wouldn't have been able to give it away.

I knew that although I'd need to once again take commercial flights to my meetings, the inconvenience would be temporary. God had just directed me to sow a significant seed; therefore, He had something even better for me.

As I said, commitment oftentimes comes with hardship. There were times in the early days of my ministry when I'd get home at two o'clock in the morning and then have to leave again the next morning. I'd awaken Jerriann and Terri in the morning and say, "Daddy's home." They'd ask how long I'd be with them, and I'd say, "Just a couple of hours. I'm getting ready to leave now."

One time when I got home, Jerriann said, "Daddy, when you left on the last trip, Terri and I gave you away."

I said, "What do you mean by that?"

She explained, "The Bible says give and it shall be given to you."

I didn't understand what she meant, so I asked, "Are you believing for another daddy?"

"No, Daddy," she giggled. " Just more time with the one we have."

In the beginning of the ministry, our entire family endured some hard times. But the commitment we made as a family has led us to a lifestyle of enjoying God's best. God's maximum. The highest level attainable.

God never asks us to give something to put us in a place of need. He asks us to give so that He can bless us with His best.

GENEROSITY BRINGS PROSPERITY

One of the greatest joys for me and Carolyn comes when we discover an opportunity to sow. Recently God has been directing us to restaurants where our servers have had great personal needs.

None of these men and women ever said a word to us about their situations, but the Lord did. We gave as He directed us, and we heard the most amazing testimonies. Giving should be the most natural act for Christians. God so loved that He gave. We so love, and we give.

One woman who served us had a sweet disposition and a wonderful attitude. She was one of the friendliest ladies we'd ever encountered, and she went above and beyond in taking care of us.

When she presented us with the bill, I added a $100 tip to it. When she saw what I'd done, she cried. She said, "You have no idea. God has been so good to me. I'm a single parent and I couldn't pay my rent this month. God just used you to help me."

How good it felt to know Carolyn and I heard from God, and our obedience to bless that woman prevented misfortune in her life.

When our server returned with the receipt, I said, "We notice you gave credit to God for this blessing. We want you to know that He is the God of more than enough." And then we gave her an additional $400 in cash.

I'm confident that the blessing she received from us was more than what she usually took home in a day. Yet it can't compare with the joy and happiness it gave me and Carolyn.

The Bible says, *"There is one who scatters, yet increases more; and there is one who withholds more than is right, but it leads to poverty"* (Proverbs 11:24). The Passion Translation says, *"Generosity brings prosperity, but withholding from charity brings poverty."* And it adds, *"Those who live to bless others will have blessings heaped upon them"* (verse 25). These verses do not describe a one-time event. Rather, they describe a committed lifestyle of generosity.

The world in which we live, with all its chaos and disorder, has become a distraction to many Christians, including those who've made the commitment to put God first and give anything He asks of them. They reason, *I'm willing to give, but these are hard times and I need to hold on to what I have.* We do live in hard times, but this is not the time to back away from our commitment to God.

Never stop giving because of circumstances. Some may say, "But, Brother Jerry, I just can't give like I used to." This may be true for now, but the situation is temporary. Don't stop giving entirely. Generosity is directly linked to prosperity.

God expects more from us than a half-hearted commitment. When it comes to following Jesus, it must be according to His words in Matthew 22:37: *"You shall love the LORD your God with all your heart, with all your soul, and with all your mind."*

Jesus also said, *"These people draw near to Me with their mouth, and honor Me with their lips, but their heart is far from Me"* (Matthew 15:8). The Passion Translation says, *"They pretend to worship me, but their worship is nothing more than the empty traditions of men"* (verse 9).

We should each examine our lives and our commitment to God. If we find we've become distracted and have drawn back from our original commitment, then it's time to act. We need to stir ourselves up.

When we put God first in our lives, then we are willing to give anything that He might ask with unbridled joy. The Bible says, *"So let each one give as he purposes in his heart, not grudgingly or of necessity; for God loves a cheerful giver"* (2 Corinthians 9:7). The Amplified Bible, Classic Edition, says, *"God loves (He takes pleasure in, prizes above other things, and is unwilling to abandon or to do without) a cheerful (joyous, "prompt to do it") giver [whose heart is in his giving]."* It goes on to say, *"And God is able to make all grace abound toward you, that you, always having all sufficiency in all things, may have an abundance for every good work*" (verse 8 NKJV).

What a promise! Sounds like the maximum, the highest level attainable. And giving is what qualifies us for God's maximum.

CHAPTER 8

FERVENT FOR GOD

David is often referred to as "a man after God's own heart" (see 1 Samuel 13:14). Despite his flaws, he exemplified qualities that we should have as followers of Jesus.

One of those qualities was that he worshipped God continually, in good times and in bad. For instance, when David wrote Psalm 34, he was running for his life. Yet he began with these words: *"I will bless the LORD at all times, His praise will continually be in my mouth"* (verse 1).

The word *praise* in this verse is the Hebrew word *halal,* which means "to be clamorously foolish about the adoration of God." To *halal* God is to praise him with passion and fervency.

It is with this fervency that David wrote these words: *"⁸O taste and see that the LORD is good; blessed is the man that trusteth in Him. ⁹O fear the LORD, ye His saints: for there is no want to them that fear him.* ¹⁰*The young lions do lack, and suffer hunger: but they that seek the LORD shall not want any good thing"* (Psalm 34:8-10 KJV). THE MESSAGE paraphrase uses the term "God seekers." God seekers shall have no want.

God seekers have made an unwavering commitment to God. Theirs is a lifestyle that qualifies them to experience God's maximum and highest level attainable. It is in that place that they have no want.

Psalm 34 is a strong call to action, a challenge for us to fully engage in seeking God continually. Not just when things get tough, but every day of our lives. People tend to cry out to God when they are in trouble, but when things are going well, their need for God calms and they become indifferent.

This indifference was one of Israel's greatest sins. When they experienced abundance, when they had everything they needed, they no longer needed God. True God seekers seek Him when things are falling apart, and they seek Him when things are going well.

They seek and serve Him every day of their lives. This is the reason they will get to the place that they have no want. These are the people who will experience the maximum and the highest level attainable.

Many Christians want God's best, but they are unwilling to do what is required to attain it. God wants each of us to get to the highest level attainable. But it isn't just going to happen. If it were possible to live at all times enjoying God's maximum, and live any old way we want to live, then all Christians would be there. But that's not the way God works.

The Word of God says, *"Those who walk along his paths with integrity will never lack one thing they need, for He provides it all!"* (Psalm 84:11 TPT). The word *integrity* in this verse implies genuineness. In other words, those who walk with God in genuineness will reach the place where they never lack one thing. We could say they don't play religious games. They don't play church. They are sincere in their love of God. They respect Him and are grateful for all He's done for them.

Psalm 92 is an expression of praise to God for His love and faithfulness. *"¹It's so enjoyable to come before you with uncontainable praises spilling from our hearts! How we love to sing our praises over and over to You, to the matchless God, high and exalted over all! ²At each and every sunrise we will be thanking You for Your kindness and your love. As the sun sets and all through the night, we will keep proclaiming, 'You are so faithful!' "* (verses 1–2 TPT).

Here is another great promise from The Passion Translation: *"Shout in celebration of praise to the Lord! Everyone who loves the Lord and delights in Him will cherish His words and be blessed beyond expectation"* (Psalm 112:1). Doesn't this sound like the maximum, the highest level attainable?

So, let me ask you a few questions. Will the prophetic word about God's Maximum, the highest level attainable, come to pass in your life? Do you qualify for it to come to pass? Are you one of the people we've been reading about who is deeply committed, passionate, unwavering, and not looking for an opportunity to quit? If you answered *yes* to these questions, then you are about to enter into one of the greatest seasons of your life. God is going to take you to the maximum and you're going to experience the highest level attainable.

Joshua said to the people of his day, "'*Now therefore, fear the LORD, serve Him in sincerity and in truth, and put away the gods which your fathers served on the other side of the River and in Egypt. Serve the LORD!*'" (Joshua 24:14). THE MESSAGE paraphrase says, "*Worship Him in total commitment.*" And here's some good advice from the Apostle Paul. He says to be "*fervent in spirit, serving the Lord*" (Romans 12:10–11).

The word *fervent* means "earnest; in pursuit; zealous intent." In modern vernacular it means "on fire." To be fervent in spirit is to be on fire for God. The Amplified Bible, Classic Edition, translation of Romans 12:11 says, "*...be aglow and burning with the Spirit, serving the Lord.*" THE MESSAGE paraphrase says, "*Don't burn out; keep yourselves fueled and aflame.*" The Passion Translation says, "*Be enthusiastic to serve the Lord, keeping your passion toward Him boiling hot! Radiate with the glow of the Holy Spirit and let Him fill you with excitement as you serve Him.*

Believers who are on fire for God are fervent in the spirit. They are excited about their walk with Him. They are also willing to do whatever He asks them to do, to give away whatever He asks to be given away. They are qualified to experience God's maximum, the highest level attainable.

GOD IS OUR INSPIRATION

As we studied God's way of doing things in chapter 6, we examined the fivefold blessing He bestowed on mankind when He created them, found in Genesis 1:26–28. But now let's go to the second chapter of Genesis and the account of His *forming* the first man. "*And the LORD God formed man of the dust of the dust of the ground, and breathed into his nostrils the breath of life; and man became a living being*" (Genesis 2:7).

The word *breathed* in this verse is symbolic of inspiration. It means "arouse to life." To be roused to life is to be inspired. It is evident that, from the very beginning, when God breathed the breath of life into the first man's nostrils, that He wanted to be mankind's inspiration. He wanted to be the reason we would rouse to life.

We could say that God's first act after forming the first man was to inspire and influence him. This influence from God was His will for us from the beginning. It is His will to this day. God wants to be our influence, the main source of our inspiration.

I like being inspired and influenced by God. One definition of *inspire* is "to communicate divine instruction." To *influence* is "to move on or to direct by an unseen power." For believers, that unseen power comes from God through the Holy Spirit.

Jesus said, "*However, when He, the Spirit of truth, has come, He will guide you into all truth ... and He will tell you things to come*" (John 16:13). A lot of time had passed from the events of Genesis to the writing of the book of John. Yet Jesus talked about His desire for mankind to be influenced by God through the Holy Spirit.

Every one of us is on our own path in life because we were influenced by someone to take that path. My first influencer was my father, my dad. I loved him and I wanted to be everything he was. I wanted to do everything he did. I wanted him to teach me everything he knew. I had a father, and I had a dad. My father and my dad, who were one in the same, was also my best friend.

I wish every boy could have a dad like mine. Most of my classmates wished they had my dad because he was a joy to be with. He loved being with me and my friends, and we loved him being with us. My dad was my primary influencer.

When I was about six or seven years old, I walked into his bedroom early one evening and found him putting on his softball uniform. He played on the team at Howard Crumley Chevrolet, the company he worked for. I already thought my dad was the biggest and strongest person in the world, but when I saw him put on that uniform I was captivated. I thought, *One day I'm going to wear a uniform like that. One day I'm going to play ball just like my dad.*

We'd always go out to the game together, and I got to carry his glove. At the ball field I got to sit in the dugout with the players. When it was time for Dad to play first base, I'd hand him his glove and he'd run onto the field.

I could hardly wait to be old enough to start Little League baseball. My best friend, Kenny Hennard, who lived across the street from me, and I were on the same team—the Brookwood Indians. At our first game I played in the outfield. But the coaches soon discovered I could pitch, so they made me the pitcher. That's the position I played throughout my school days and then into the farm league, sponsored by the Kansas City Royals.

My dad had once told me he would never miss one of my games, and he was true to his word. Sometimes he had to take off work to attend an afternoon game. I could hear him shouting from the stands, "Strike him out, Bubba. Strike him out!"

My mom also attended games, mostly those at night. I especially remember one game. I threw my first pitch and—whack!—a big ole boy hit it over the fence behind center field for a home run. My mother stood up and yelled, "A home run! Wow, a home run!" My dad said, "Sit down Attie. It's the wrong team."

My dad was also the inspiration for my love of old cars, fast cars, hot rods, and motorcycles. He taught me how to work on them, how to build them, how to drive them. I've often said my dad saw to it that I never owned a slow vehicle or motorcycle. He modified everything I drove or rode so that I could outrun everyone else.

Eventually I opened my own automotive business, Jerry's Paint and Body Shop, where I applied all the skills I'd learned from my dad. I was living my dream.

But then, in 1969, another influencer came into my life. His name was Kenneth Copeland. Of course, I still loved my dad, but he didn't know what Kenneth Copeland knew. Kenneth Copeland knew about the things of God, and at the time I was running from God as hard and fast as I could.

I'd known from the day I watched Oral Roberts on my grandmother's old black-and-white television that I had the call of God on my life. But I didn't want any part of it. Kenneth Copeland was the man God used to inspire and influence me to begin to follow God's dream for my life instead of the dream I'd created for my own life.

I've been in the ministry for more than fifty years, and Brother Copeland and I have been preaching together for all but two of those years. He still inspires me. He still influences me. During my years in ministry, I've also been inspired by Oral Roberts, Kenneth Hagin, and T.L. Osborn. These three men, who've each gone to be with the Lord, each helped shape me and my ministry.

I'm now privileged to know that I've inspired young ministers all over the world. Many consider me a spiritual father. That's not something I set out to become. In my mind, I'm just Jerry Savelle.

Each one of us—regardless of our individual path—is where we are because someone influenced us. Someone inspired us. For this reason, we must use wisdom when forming relationships and friendships. The Bible says, *"He who walks with wise men will be wise, but the companion of fools will be destroyed"* (Proverbs 13:20). THE MESSAGE paraphrase says, *"Become wise by walking with the wise; hang out with fools and watch your life fall to pieces."*

People have a way of inspiring us, whether for good or bad. Brother Hagin used to say, "You can imbibe another man's spirit." To *imbibe* means "to absorb or assimilate." This is the reason we are to connect with people of "like precious faith," a term used in 2 Peter 1:1. We are to run with people who sharpen us according to Proverbs 27:17: *"As iron sharpens iron, so a man sharpens the countenance of his friend."*

God should always be our primary source of inspiration, but He also uses people who are filled with His Spirit to inspire and influence us as we walk out our commitment to serve Him.

GOD BREATHES ON COVENANT RELATIONSHIPS

When Brother Copeland first launched his Victory Campaigns, the Lord gave me some specific instructions about those meetings. So, I went to talk to him about those instructions.

"Brother Copeland, I will be at all your Victory Campaigns this year. I want to serve you and do whatever you need me to do. I'll pay my own expenses. Though I have my own ministry, I want to give a portion of my time to you and your ministry. I want to support you as I always have."

He said, "Jerry, if you are there, don't think you're not going to preach."

"No, sir, Brother Copeland. I don't have to preach. I'm coming to lift your hands, to serve you, and do what I need to do to help you."

Brother Copeland was firm in his response. "You *will* preach if you're coming with me."

"Okay," I said. "But I don't want an offering. I'm sowing my time as a seed."

I was at every Victory Campaign that year, and I paid my own way. I was there to serve, and that's what I did. In my mind, I was going to do this for one year. But at the end of that year the Lord asked, "Would you be willing to do this for the rest of your life?"

I said *yes,* and then I made a new commitment to Brother Copeland. "I will do these Victory Campaigns as long as you want me to for the rest of my life." That commitment overwhelmed him. I have kept that commitment all these years. It is a form of giving.

Giving my time to Brother Copeland and serving him has not hurt my ministry at all, despite sometimes doing two campaigns in a month. Not receiving finances from him for my service has not hurt my ministry's finances. If anything, my ministry has gone to another level. This kind of giving is a lifestyle for me. It is the reason I experience the maximum and the highest level attainable.

Recently, as Brother Copeland and I were flying to a meeting, he put his arm around me and said, "I love you, Son."

I responded, "I love you, Dad." Though we are only ten years apart in age, I consider him my spiritual father, and he considers me his spiritual son.

But then he said something that overwhelmed me. "Jerry, you're the brother I never had." Those seven words really got to me. The reason is that Brother Copeland is an only child. His mother almost died giving birth to him, and she was unable to have more children. He'd always wanted a brother.

Brother Copeland and I have been in a God-ordained relationship for more than fifty years. I am on the path I'm on today because he influenced me to follow the Lord and His plan for my life. God has truly breathed His influence and inspiration on this covenant relationship that has touched countless lives throughout the world.

One of the greatest joys in my life is the way in which the Lord allowed me to influence my dad in his latter years. He had been my greatest childhood influencer, but then, when I started my ministry, he and my mother moved to Texas and worked with me for twenty years.

Every time God did something for me, my dad was one of the first ones I wanted to tell. I can't count the times I said, "Dad, look what the Lord has done!" He'd put his hands out towards me and say, "You're blessed, boy. You're truly blessed."

He was right. And I was blessed to be my parents' influence and their inspiration until they each went home to be with the Lord.

I've also been blessed to enjoy friendships with others who revere and honor God as I do. David said it this way, *"I am a companion of all who fear You, and of those who keep Your precepts"* (Psalm 119:63). Godly friends are needful in the world we live in today. The Bible says, *"Do not be deceived, 'Evil company corrupts good habits'"* (1 Corinthians 15:33). The Amplified Bible, Classic Edition, says, *"Evil companionships (communion, associations) corrupt and deprave good manners and morals and character."*

It's important who we choose as our companions because, as the saying goes, "you become the company you keep." I heard one preacher say, "Show me your friends and I'll show you your character."

Earlier in this chapter we learned that, in the beginning, God breathed the breath of life into the first man. Now let's look at something the risen Jesus did just before He took His position at the right hand of God. *So Jesus said to them again, [21]"'Peace to you! As the Father has sent Me, I also send you.' [22]And when He had said this, He breathed on them, and said to them, 'Receive the Holy Spirit'"* (John 20:21–22).

When Jesus commissioned His disciples, He did the same thing to them that God did when He created mankind,

107

He breathed on them. In essence, Jesus was saying, "I want to be to you what God intended from the beginning—your inspiration and your influence."

Now let's go to the book of Acts and see what happened after Jesus said, "Receive the Holy Spirit." "*And suddenly there came a sound from heaven, as of a rushing mighty wind, and it filled the whole house where they were sitting*" (Acts 2:2). The Holy Spirit is oftentimes referred to as the "wind of God." When we receive the Holy Spirit, it's God's way of breathing on us once again.

For this reason, we need to stay close to God. We need to draw nigh unto Him. We need to stay on fire for Him.

God's breathing on us, just as He breathed on the believers in the book of Acts, signifies we will be inspired and influenced by God. The Holy Spirit is the breath of God. Once we have received the Holy Spirit, then God's influence and inspiration never cease. And it is *that* inspiration and influence that will take us to the maximum, the highest level attainable.

I invite you now to join me, and pray this prayer out loud:

Heavenly Father,

In the name of Jesus, I ask You to cause the flames of fire to rise within me. Cause the fire to grow higher, that I may burn brighter for You. Let this be for me a moment of fresh commitment to You and Your plan for my life.

Holy Spirit, breathe upon me. Inspire and influence me all the days of my life.

Father, rouse me to new life from this day forward in the mighty name of Jesus.

You said if I will draw nigh to You, You will draw nigh to me. I now draw nigh to You, knowing You will honor Your Word to me.

I thank You, Father, that You have heard my prayer. Your Word in Job 22:28 says that I will decide and decree a thing, and it will be established for me, and the light of Your favor will shine upon my ways. Therefore, I now decree that I am inspired by the Holy Spirit, and that the fire of God rises upon me to take me to new heights. I burn and glow with the presence of God both now and all the days of my life. I receive all God has for me—the maximum, the highest level attainable.

In Jesus name. Amen.

ABOUT THE AUTHOR

Dr. Jerry Savelle was an average, blue-collar man who struggled and needed God's help. While he considered himself a "nobody," when he became a believer, God told him not to worry about it because He was a master at making champions out of nobodies. God has since taken Dr. Savelle from being a constant quitter to a man who knows how to stand on the Word of God until victory is experienced. Because of the life-changing combination of God's faithfulness and Dr. Savelle's "no quit" attitude, his life is totally different than it was fifty years ago.

Since 1969, Dr. Savelle has been traveling the world, teaching people how to win in life. Dr. Savelle has ministered in over thirty-five hundred churches in over forty nations and has overseas offices in the United Kingdom, Australia, Canada, and South Africa, as well as numerous Bible Schools in several nations.

God has used Dr. Savelle to inspire people worldwide, to take hold of the promises of God and become the winners in life that God has called them to be, and to become a testimony to His faithfulness.

He hosts the Jerry Savelle Ministries television broadcast in two hundred countries around the world. He is the author of more than seventy books, including his bestsellers –"If Satan Can't Steal Your Joy, He Can't Keep Your Goods" and "Called to Battle, Destined to Win." He and his wife, Carolyn, also serve as founding pastors of Heritage of Faith Christian Center in Crowley, Texas.

Other best-selling books by Dr. Jerry Savelle

- *From Devastation to Restoration*
- *The Favor of God*
- *Called to Battle, Destined to Win*
- *The God of the Breakthrough Will Visit Your House*
- *In the Footsteps of a Prophet*
- *Prayer of Petition*

For additional information about
Jerry Savelle Ministries International
visit our website at jerrysavelle.org.